Lost in a Game:
The Road to Self Discovery

Maria Young

Lost in a Game: The Journey to Self Discovery

Produced by:
NyreePress Literary Group
Fort Worth, TX 76161
1-800-972-3864
www.nyreepress.com

Interior Design: www.doodles.blue

ISBN print: 978-1-945304-47-7

Library of Congress Control Number: pending
Categories: Non-Fiction / Memoir
Printed in the United States of America

"Creativity is an energy. It's a precious energy, and it's something to be protected. A lot of people take for granted that they're a creative person, but I know from experience, feeling it in myself, it is a magic; it is an energy. And it can't be taken for granted."

Ava DuVernay

"When you learn, teach. When you get, give."

Maya Angelou

"There is no better than adversity. Every defeat, every heartbreak, every loss, contains its own seed, its own lesson on how to improve your performance the next time."

Malcolm X

Table of Contents

1

Signing Day

April 21, 2009 was a day I'd dreamed of as a young child growing up in Asheville, North Carolina. It was the day I was able to choose which institution of higher learning would receive my talent and its entire splendor. The seats in the gymnasium of TC Roberson High School were filled with my family, friends, and teammates. Beside me, sat my best friend and teammate of thirteen years, as we had decided to hold our press conference together, displaying our last stand of solidarity as high school teammates. In front of me was a National Letter Of Intent to play college basketball. I glanced over at my mother, who was sitting to my left, and observed tears in her eyes. The countless hours of carting me to practices and all the money she'd put into my AAU tournaments, high school games, uniforms, basketball shoes, club fees, and travel expenses directly led to this moment.

I was mere seconds away from signing my name on the dotted line to have my education paid for, while continuing to play the game I had devoted myself to. My mother leaned over and swept me into her embrace, never saying a word, but I knew she was proud of where I was in that moment. I kissed her on the cheek, put my head on her shoulder, closed my eyes, and said a quick prayer. *"Dear God, thank you for my talent, thank you for my mother, and thanks for this opportunity. Amen."* I picked up the pen and signed my name across the dotted line, committing myself to Limestone College, an up and coming Division II program in Gaffney, South Carolina; eighty-seven miles south of my hometown. I lifted my contract up and shook it in the air to indicate that it was now official. The gym irrupted in cheers as everyone descended upon the scorer's table. I heard everything from, "Go make history!" to, "Don't come back to Asheville!" to, "Don't squander this opportunity!" and lastly, "Make sure they remember your name when you leave." But, the one thing I never heard was, "Don't forget the real reason you are there." The absence of those words proved to be in direct correlation with the path my life was beginning to take.

2

Graduation

I rolled over in bed as I was awakened by laughter and the smell of my grandmother's Saturday morning breakfast. When I opened my eyes, I smiled, feeling a true sense of accomplishment. It was my graduation day. Later that evening, I was going to walk across a stage in front of hundreds of people, smile, shake my principal's hand, and receive my high school diploma. I sat up and observed my room. The walls were riddled with plaques and trophies I'd received from a bevy of basketball accomplishments. Just as I picked up my MVP trophy from the dresser, a wave of fear washed through my body. I was fearful of the future, the unknown, and of what I would become.

Being regarded as one of the best point guards in Western North Carolina provided me a sense of security and comfort. I knew, in this city, I was the best and everyone loved me for my athletic ability. I brought joy to people when I put on a TC Roberson jersey and left my heart on the floor. Having to step out of that amenity, and not knowing if I would have the same prosperity at Limestone, was unsettling. The day my high school team lost in the semi-finals of the state tournament, I cried for three days straight, because I knew that glorious chapter of my life was over. I didn't know if I would ever feel that triumph through basketball again. *Without the game, what am I?*

As I got dressed and entered the kitchen I observed my mother, grandmother, older brother, aunts, and uncles enjoying breakfast and engaged in a seemingly hilarious conversation. Growing up in a tight-knit family was one of the true treasures of my life. We seldom had a weekend that we were not at my grandmother's home in Shiloh, relishing each other's company. Before I go any further, to understand me is to first understand my love and pride of where I came from. Shiloh is a middle to lower class African American community located in south Asheville. My grandmother has lived in her home for forty-four years, much like many of the elders in our community. Shiloh has a way of making you feel like royalty through the continual love and support of one another. This neighborhood is my village and being able to say I'm from Shiloh is equivalent to being showered with all the riches the world has to offer.

My family instilled the 'triple F' philosophy in my older brother, cousins, and me at a young age. Triple F stands for Faith, Family, and Fellowship. Faith: Believing that God is the orchestrator of all things. He is your guide. He is your light, and He can deliver you from any doubt or dark place you may find yourself in. Family: Our tribe, blood, and childhood friends. Never forgetting who will pick you up when you fall and lift you up higher when you succeed. Fellowship: The time spent and memories created with people who mean the most to you. Every single person in that kitchen had a direct hand in guiding me to this graduation day.

I grabbed a plate and sat at the small round kitchen table—which is suited for four, but currently sat eight. I had a moment of reflection as I viewed each member of my family. My mother—words could never express my appreciation for her life, her countless sacrifices, and the foundation she built on faith, family, and fellowship. I couldn't have made it to graduation day without her unconditional love and guidance. My grandmother, who's wisdom and life stories proved to have a deeper impact on me than I'd realized in this moment. She allowed my mother and me to move in with her for a while to assist my mother with her financial challenges. If this move had not happened, God only knows where my basketball career would be. My older brother was a sophomore in college at the time. Our relationship was one of distance, but I appreciated the example he was setting for me. My aunties showered me with love and spoiled me more than I deserved. I could do no wrong in their eyes. Last, but not least, my uncles. They had served as my tribe of father figures and protected me as if I was their own child. The gratitude I feel for these people is overwhelming, and I hide my face in my plate before anyone can notice the water in my eyes and the tremble of my lips.

After a few hours of conversation and setting up for my graduation cookout, I got dressed and we headed to the venue. Our neighbor, who lived across the street, detailed limos for a living and was able to pull a few strings so my family and I could be driven to my graduation in style. You couldn't tell us anything. We dressed to kill, in our "Sunday's best"—as my grandmother stated and "Fresh as new napkins," as my uncle relayed. The windows were rolled down, the sunroof was pushed back, the black national anthem (as I call it) Frankie Beverley and Maze 'Before I Let Go' was softly playing in the background, and my family and I were singing along with the words. We were just happy to be in the presence of one another and even happier to be celebrating this milestone.

While everyone was enjoying the ride, my mother was staring out her window with a concerned expression. When I asked if she was okay, she told me that she was fine, but that she has a request of me. She stated that she wants me to be respectful to my father, as he would be joining us at the graduation. I agreed, although everything within me wanted to disobey my mother's wishes. You have probably wondered why I haven't mentioned my father up until this point. The reason is, our relationship is very complex, and one that is a tumultuous ride of emotion. My mother and father were briefly married when I was younger. When they divorced, he would still come around, and we spent time together some weekends. Well... let me rephrase that. He would pick me up, and I would spend time at his house with him, his new wife's children, and their friends. The majority of these weekends were not enjoyable, but as a child, you learn how to entertain yourself. A few of his step children were older than I was, as were their friends. More often than not, I was shooting basketball outside or sitting around watching television or watching the older kids play video games.

Although I was welcomed in their home, I never felt like I fit in or belonged there. I was reserved and opted to stay to myself until I was asked to do something. I felt like an outcast, hanging out with unfamiliar people whom I had a large age difference with. I became more vocal in my opposition about going to my father's home, for more reasons than what you see depicted above.

As I got older, I started to notice that he was not coming to my youth league games or my AAU tournaments. I stopped being excited about the gifts he would buy, realizing I never actually cared about the gifts; I only cared about spending time with my dad and feeling supported by him. In middle school, I started to notice that my mom and dad's interactions were always negative. 'If looks could kill' glances were common and phone calls always turned into arguments. I vividly remember one night (before my grandmother allowed us to move in with her), my mom was sitting at our dining room table. I was supposed to be asleep, but the raising of my mother's voice as she took a phone call startled me. I snuck to my door and eavesdropped on her conversation. The following statements never faded in my memory.

"I can't keep doing all of this by myself. Being her father is more than a few weekends here and there. I have two mouths to feed. I called because I need your help. Fine, I will figure it out on my own." As my mother hung up, she picked up a pen and pulled a calculator close to her. I recognized that she was trying to figure out how we could afford to go to an upcoming AAU tournament. My mother never directly discussed our money problems with me, but I noticed at AAU tournaments, she would send me to eat with my team and tell me she wasn't hungry. Or, upon returning from a tournament, our cable would be off, and things that were not necessities were completely scaled back. This conversation was the first confirmation I had that my mom was not receiving assistance from my dad, and I surrendered to my feelings of desertion. A seed was planted in the corner of my heart that blossomed into resentment.

"DAD"

When did our bond begin to flee?

When did we start to disagree?

When did I stop being your little girl?

Why did I become equivalent to a fatherless child in the world?

You were supposed to be my first love.

The first man I should have been in awe of

The first man to remind me of ALL I was

Days turned into months

Months into years

Eventually, I dried my tears.

Resentment grew

The love you gave your steps, I wish I knew

You love me when it's beneficial for you

Supported me once my name grew

The good book says I'm supposed to honor and forgive you

Problem is, I don't know how too.

I stopped worrying about if he was going to be at a game. I stopped looking for his phone call. I stopped wanting his gifts, and I stopped yearning for his support. Everyone around me knew basketball was like air to me, and I could not understand why my parent would not attempt to encourage me in any way he could. As time went on, we had little to no communication for long periods of time, and I observed a pattern beginning to form. If I had a write up in the paper about me as a basketball player, a call would come. If he heard praise from someone about a great game I had or how exceptional I was as a player, a call would come. If he felt that I was not appreciative of what he "tried" to do because I did not mention his name or acknowledge him in any success I had, a call would come. My mom tried to encourage me to build a relationship with my dad, despite her personal feelings, but she understood I was old enough to make that decision on my own. I felt my dad only wanted a true relationship when my name was beneficial to him. Although I never doubted his love, his aid and support were void, and I doubted if he was authentic and trustworthy. We no longer had a bond. We did not have much of a relationship, and he felt like my father in name only. Although it was my graduation day, I was not thrilled he would be there.

We arrived at the venue. I kissed my family and told them we would meet out front after the ceremony. I acknowledged my father, and then met up with my '09 crew. I rarely called my '09 crew my friends because "friends" is an inadequate way to describe our connection. They were my family, a part of my tribe and my village. We had been inseparable since elementary and middle school, and every memory I have worth sharing has one of these people a part of it. We reflected on all the wild, crazy, and fun times we shared with one another and established an understanding that these relationships would continue to be cultivated once we went to college. We shared a group hug and proceeded to our places as the ceremony was about to start.

As our names were being called, we were ecstatic for one another as each of us crossed the stage and received our diploma. We were told prior to the ceremony to hold our applause until the end, but how many black folks do you know that actually abide by that request? Don't worry, I'll wait... Once the ceremony concluded, I found my family again and was showered with congratulatory hugs and kisses. After my aunt had taken a million pictures (as she always did) we finally made our way back to my grandmother's home. I saw that my uncles and a lot of folks from the neighborhood had already gathered in the yard. One uncle was on the grill, another was in charge of the music, and a number of party-goers had already begun dancing. More and more people joined the festivities, while people in cars passed by yelling, "Congratulations on Limestone" and "Make Shiloh proud."

As I was visiting with each person at the cookout, I was approached by a friend of the neighborhood. We engaged in a conversation that placed one more step on the athletic pedestal that had been built over my lifetime. He told me that it indeed was a great accomplishment to graduate high school, but now I was in a position to "really do something special." He stated that I had the opportunity to go "anywhere my talent could take me" and basketball was going to be my "ticket to achieving great things." This was the type of praise I had become accustomed to. Hearing that recognition was equivalent to a junkie receiving another fix of their favorite drug.

I began playing basketball at the age of six, and from the day I picked up a ball for the first time, it was obvious that I was better than the majority of the children I played with and against. From the age of six, all I heard was how great I was on a basketball court; and the foundation of the pedestal I currently stood on was established. Each game, a new brick was laid, and after each accolade, a new step was built. My identity and feelings were simultaneous with the bounce of a ball and the sound of a swish. After this conversation with my friend, the fear and anxiety I felt graduation morning subsided when the rave of my basketball skill invaded my hearing and slipped into my veins.

3

Moving on Up

Selecting the perfect college was a critical decision for me, but not for the reasons you may think. For most students, you want to choose a college or university that coincides with your academic and future career aspirations. You consider what programs and majors the institution offers, location, academic scholarships, financial aid assistance, admission criteria, class size, and career opportunities. You want to be able to join a school that will not only teach you academically, but also equip you with the professional skills necessary to be successful post-graduation.

I, on the other hand, made the common mistake that so many young athletes make, and that was solely considering what the college could do for me athletically. Prior to signing my Letter of Intent, a few additional colleges and universities including a mid-major Division 1 university extended offers to me. Each of these schools had a draw back for me athletically, ranging from rumored coaching changes to playing behind juniors and seniors and not being able to have an immediate impact on the court. Limestone was a program that was being rebuilt into relevancy, and it was on track to establishing itself as a Conference Carolina and NCAA tournament contender. Limestone fused veteran pieces with supremely talented youth to construct something special, possibly legendary. The type of offensive system Limestone established was tailor-made for a player with my skill set. I had no hesitations or reservations about entrusting myself to these coaches. The process was just beginning.

The morning of move-in day was very emotional for my family as I was their baby and officially the last one to head to college. I left my home and hugged my grandmother's neck, fighting back tears as she began to cry too. She told me how much she loved me and exhausted that I always "do the right thing." Our car was packed tight with my belongings. Accompanied by my mother and aunts, we headed to Gaffney, South Carolina. On our way down the mountain, I was wrestling with myself in an attempt to contain my emotions. I knew my life was about to change. I wanted to cry. The sense of unfamiliarity and anxiety was almost unbearable.

I am a reserved, bashful, and kind of anti-social introvert, who does not enjoy meeting new people or associating with many individuals outside of my family and teammates. I get very nervous conversing with new individuals, and I am genuinely uncomfortable having unnecessary "small talk" conversations. I just half-heartedly smile and offer single word replies in an effort to conceal as much of my personal feelings and thoughts as possible, hoping that the conversation ceases not long after it starts. Why, you ask? I am insecure enough to believe that very few human beings are able to organically connect with the few, outdated interests I carry. I am star athlete who adores the soulful sounds of the golden era of 70's soul music, who watches films and television shows religiously, picking screenplays a part and taking notice of who is writing and producing each project, and who reads poetry for fun. *Will I seem pure, or will I be perceived as another person trying too hard to be different?*

My complexities as an individual frightened me as I struggled to understand where they stemmed from; so, I know a complete stranger would not understand either. In this moment, I reinforced the brick walls and electric fences around what I deemed to be the best parts of me: my intelligence, my aspirations, my passions, and my heart.

PROFUSION

Abundance to give

Yet, shackled by fear

Fear of acceptance

Fear of the unknown

The absence of fear is the absence of growth

Yearning to stand secure in my being

Without validation that it's enough

Revealing the depths of introspection

Praying for genuine connections

Yet, vulnerably I cannot give

This means I cannot live

When we arrived on campus and began unpacking the car, I emerged from my thoughts as I was greeted by my new teammates. Once they introduced themselves, my emotions began to calm because I felt safe. These were the young ladies that I would be going to battle with and the people who shared common interests and goals through basketball—the center of my universe. As we continued to unpack and set up my room, I remained present in this moment with my family, as I knew they would be leaving me in a few hours. We shared an abundance of laughs as they stocked my dorm room with items I would never use or need. They hung up collages of our countless parties and times of fellowship together, cleaned my bathroom, and made my bed for me. This was the way they moved my brother and cousins in before me, and I was no exception to the tradition.

Once they were done, the realization set in for everyone and my aunts began to cry as they embraced me one last time. I fought the internal pull of wanting to sob because I wanted to assure them that I was going to be okay; although the concern in my soul was stifling. My mother, whose intuition sensed that I was scared, asked my aunts to meet her at the car. She pulled me into one of her strong hugs. I allowed all of my emotions to overflow as I wept on her shoulder. One of my mother's finest attributes was illustrated in this moment. Her ability to reassure. I distinctly remember my mother telling me that it was "okay to be afraid" and that I had a golden opportunity to continue playing the game I loved while bettering my education. She left me with a phrase she continues to use to this day. "Remember, God has you here for a reason."

I pondered my mother's words once she left my dorm room. *What is my reason for being here?* Instead of praying and asking for clarity from my higher power, I applied my own interpretation to those words. *What is the one thing I am truly good at? What is the one thing that the people surrounding me recognize me for?* One thing, basketball.

4

A New World

Months into my freshman year, my separation anxiety had ceased, and I was continuing to acclimate in this new environment. Although the general transition of meeting my advisor, getting my course schedule, and finding where classes were held went smoothly, I was still a bit reclusive. I automatically made connections with my teammates, but bonding with anyone outside of that circle was more of a challenge. I forced myself to have some of those small talk conversations, but I quickly realized that it just made both parties much more uncomfortable. Academically, I had not yet begun to take courses related to my major, so my class schedule was not overwhelmingly difficult. The only problem was my old habits were never corrected. In fact, they were enhanced by my new-found freedom. Mere months into my collegiate experience, I was not attending my classes on a regular basis, nor was I meeting team academic requirements.

As a freshman, transitioning into college can be problematic. Being away from home for the first time, meeting new people, making new friends, deciding what career path to take, how to problem solve and adjust to the demands of being independent can be overwhelming. As a collegiate athlete, this transition is twice as demanding. Not only was I adjusting to new responsibilities as a student, I had the added pressure of performing on the basketball court. The initial weeks were nothing short of a struggle. I was not physically prepared for the college game and had a very hard time integrating myself into the pace of collegiate basketball. I was a shell of the player I had been up until this point. Would I be another one of those players that had a great high school career, but failed to excel on the college stage? This question dominated my mind and became all I thought about in my workouts and classes. If I couldn't perform on the basketball court, I knew there was nothing else I could be successful at, because without basketball, who was I?

One day, approximately a month before we officially started practice, my head coach pulled me aside following a terrible workout. My coach was a very intense man, who demanded every ounce of what you should give when you're in between those lines. He expected 110% every second you were on the court, and if you did not meet that expectation, he would scream and yell about your laziness until you understood the reasoning behind his expectation. What set my coach apart from all my former coaches was his ability to be acute, but mutually informative and encouraging. In this moment, he could sense that my confidence was wavering, and he felt the need to initiate a conversation about any issues I had.

First, we spoke about school—as he was fully aware of my absences and missed assignments. Coach was concerned that I was already making decisions that could be detrimental to my future this early in my college career. He asked me about my acclimation into the school, and it put me in a place of comfort. Here he was, my basketball coach, asking about me as an individual, not his player. It was the first time I recognized that I am now playing for a coach who cared about my wellbeing first. His worry allowed me to drop a layer of armor around my feelings and allow myself to express my hardships to him. I explained that my current shortcomings on the basketball court were affecting me more than I led on, and I was disappointed in myself for not living up to the player I know could be. My coach reinforced his philosophy of hard work and his belief in me, but he added that basketball was simply a "game" and that it should not affect my studies. With that, I was issued a stern warning for my missed classes and informed that another missed course would result in punishment. This conversation allowed me to see that I was surrounded by people who cared. It restored some of my confidence as well.

Days after that conversation with my coach, our team had our four-person skill development workout. My group consisted of our starting point guard—one of my fellow freshman teammates who was all but guaranteed a starting position at this point—and our starting small forward. Our skill development workouts were ultra-important because you had an opportunity to display your individual strengths to the coaching staff. With the influx of numerous recruits and incalculable game minutes waiting to be claimed, we were either fighting for a spot or fighting to retain the one we currently held. Walking into the gym that day, my spirit felt different... centered, I should say.

Skill D began and it was one filled with high energy, competitiveness, and peak physical contact. Every drill was a competition, as the loser had some sort of repercussion for coming up short. We concluded the day with one of coach's favorite drills: full court one-on-one. As expected, he placed a five-dribble limit on the offensive player—meaning, we have six dribbles to go the length of the ninety-four-foot basketball court and score on our opponent. He partnered me with the starting small forward, who was a senior and happened to be one of my closest friends at the time. In the previous season, she was Limestone's leading scorer. She was freakishly athletic, cat quick, and awkwardly enough, it was her minutes and her spot that I was striving for. Coach called our group to the baseline and placed me on defense first.

Understanding my teammate's quickness, I used my length to my advantage. This allowed me to give myself a chance to mirror her quickness, while being in the vicinity to contest her shot. This strategy worked as she could not get an angle on me to drive to the basket. Instead, I forced her into a contested jump shot (Coach's favorite)—plus one for my confidence.

It was now my opportunity to be on offense. My teammate was an exceptional defender, so my main objective was to create space to get a clean jump shot, or create space, read her reaction and counter her move. As I dribbled up the court, I got her to bite on a simple hesitation crossover, which gave me the split second I needed to slide by her to the basket for an easy layup. I glanced at my coaching staff, who were clapping and smiling about the move I'd just executed. That basket held a deeper significance than just another bucket. That basket told me that I could play at this level and that this was where I belonged. The player I had always been was still inside me and had the potential to be significantly better. My Shiloh swagger was beginning to emerge, as my attitude and slight arrogance crept to the surface. The remainder of that workout went very well. I shocked myself, and my teammates, with some of the plays I made. My coaches gave me extra pats on the back, confirming that this was the beginning of how good I could be.

This was the day that Shiloh was born. After this workout, I told everyone I knew at Limestone College that I would no longer go by Maria. From that day forward, I wanted to be addressed as Shiloh. Why, you ask? For me, it was simple. The player that was beginning to emerge was born and bred in Shiloh, North Carolina, and by saying my name, you were acknowledging the very place I came from. My teammates and fellow students complied, but my head coach did not, as he said it was "not my name." and "never expect to hear me say that". The better I played, the bigger the Shiloh persona grew. I was slowly losing myself before I had a chance to build. I created a mask to hide behind, because eventually, Shiloh was all I let anyone know and see.

Pre-season continued into official practices and each passing day, I was becoming a better basketball player. Although I was eyeing my teammates starting spot, she was not one to easily surrender. We had a few epic battles during our blue and white, inter- squad scrimmages. She was very aware that I was emerging as a top player on our team, so she made it a point to challenge me each day in practice. I received an extra push coming off a down screen, an extra pull of my jersey, and a stare down when she scored on me. What she did not realize was that the competitor inside my being thrived on trash talk and streetball-esque play. I internalized her actions and used them as motivation on the next play. There was no need for me to speak when my game alone could hold a conversation.

By the time our season opener rolled around, I'd worked my way up into the sixth man position. Although I was not starting, I was content with where I was, because I remained available to have an enormous impact on the outcome of our games.

Season Opener (First Collegiate Game): Armstrong Atlantic vs Limestone College November 15th, 2009

The morning of the season opener, I woke up to a sinking feeling in the pit of my stomach. The day had finally arrived, I was hours away from officially starting my college basketball career. I prepared myself to follow my pre-game routine to a T. This routine never changed in my four years as a player.

- Eat pre-game meal with my team three hours before tip-off.

- Ice my knees in the dorm room while watching episodes of the 'Martin' sitcom.

- Place my hands on the bible I carry in my athletic bag, saying a quick prayer before exiting for the gym.

- Arrive at the gym one hour before the team is required to be there.

- Execute my shooting routine while listening to my special "Game Day Mix," consisting of music from 2 PAC, Nas, Eric B and Rakim, 8ball and MJG, Travis Porter, Lil Wayne, Kanye West and the Shiloh Corner Boyz- ("I Do Itttt! I be at ATM, enterin' my pin!")

- Stretch fifteen minutes before the entire team.

- Retreat to the locker room five minutes before official warmups to get completely dressed.

- Place my hands on my bible again and go into one more prayer.

Throughout our warmups, I attempted to subdue my nervousness by repeating to myself, *You're here for a reason. You're here for a reason.* Although I felt prepared during our practices, this was the real moment—what truly mattered. *What are you going to do when the lights are bright and the moment is right in front of you? It's time to step up and flourish, or fade into irrelevance.* Warm ups concluded and the national anthem began to play. I lowered my head, closed my eyes, and went into my final prayer—praying for good health, praying that I seize the moment, praying I make my tribe proud, and thanking the Most High for extending this opportunity to me. *My time is now.*

A little over seven minutes tick off the clock, and we are in a tight game early. My coach finally calls my number, and I enter the game to take my place on the right wing. My teammate passes me the ball, and I immediately swing it back. The problem was, no one was there, and I threw the ball directly out of bounds. As expected, my coach pulled me out of the game and screamed at me, "What are you doing?! This a grown woman's game!" I shot him the meanest side eye I could muster as his words infuriated me. I made one mistake, and now I cannot play a "grown woman's game?" Okay…

I waited impatiently for my next opportunity to enter the game. I locked eyes with my coach on several occasions, displaying a look of, "If you don't put me back in this game, we gon' have some problems." After several more minutes, Coach finally calls my number again. He told me to relax and play my game before I reenter. I appreciated his words, but I already knew what I had to do. The game progressed for a few possessions before I got my opportunity off our opponents missed basket. My team was in transition. I filled my lane as we practiced, and our point guard forwarded a strong pass to me on the left wing. I immediately identified that I was wide open and do not hesitate to let the three-point shot go. It was all net!

The PA announcer shouted, "Maria Young for threeee!" I smiled as I glanced over to my tribe, who had irrupted in cheers. Over twenty members of my immediate family and Shiloh friends made the trip to experience my first collegiate game. In my mind, I visualized that ball going through the net and shattering the glass backboard, symbolizing the crash of the box I felt I was in as a player. Now, there were truly no limits to what I could achieve in a Limestone basketball jersey.

I finished my first collegiate game with sixteen points in twenty-one minutes, connecting on three made three-point shots. I was satisfied with my stat line for this game, but it was fulfilling to know that I was gaining my coach's trust as I remained in the game during key possessions. I knew more minutes would be coming my way; I just had to make sure I was ready to step up and succeed in them.

Five games into my freshman season, I was inserted into the starting lineup. With an average of sixteen points over our first four match ups against formidable opponents, and a string of practices in which I was simply unstoppable, Coach explained that my current play and some of our slow starts prompted him to switch things up. I smiled as my body exuded joy, but that feeling briefly halted as I began to think about my teammate and how this move could affect our friendship. As if Coach read my mind, he reassured me that she was fine with the move, as she would remain a focal point for our team. His admission eased my concern, and he continued to tell me that "the real work starts now," and I needed to continue to work hard, as this season would present a lot of challenges for a freshman.

I left that meeting and quickly called my mother to relay the good news. Of course, she had the feeling that I should have been starting since the very first game. I also admitted that I was concerned about taking the spot of someone I was very close to. I described how the feeling was bittersweet because I was starting to achieve some of my individual goals, but this one, came at the expense of a teammate that had been a sister to me in every sense of the word. Again, my mother's best quality of reassurance shined through. My mother stated that I "deserved to have this opportunity" and that I simply played the game the best way I knew how. She continued, "As for your teammate, she should be happy for you if y'all are as close as you say." My mother's words abolished any uncertainty about being named a starter. Now, I was officially ready for any obstacle this season would present. Maria "Shiloh" Young had officially arrived.

Despite basketball coming full circle, I found myself in an awful position academically. I was punished twice in my first semester for excessive absences. My punishment consisted of running sprints before or after practice for each class I missed and individual study hall sessions that took place in my coach's office. Our professors were sent bi-weekly progress reports to fill out, so my head coach could monitor our academic progress. Near the end of my first semester, I was failing two courses and had a D in another. This prompted another meeting, in which my coach told me that I was very close to being ineligible in the spring and not being able to finish my freshman season if I did not pull my D up and pass at least one of the classes I was currently failing. I was given restrictions that, under no circumstance, I couldn't miss any more classes or assignments for the remainder of the semester or I would be suspended, with additional reports sent home to my mother.

Yes, you read that right. My mother was well aware of my academic struggles; not only because she was involved in every fabric of my life, but because my coaches understood that when their words fell on deaf ears, my mother would be heard loud and clear. They would email her if a professor inquired about my whereabouts, my attitude in class, or missing grades. I received plenty of, "You're not too old for me to bust you in the back of your head" texts, and "Gaffney is an hour away. Don't make me come down there!" phone calls. If you know my mother, you are aware that she never makes an idle threat. If she said it, that was exactly what she was going to do. For all the love she gave, she had no problem being a disciplinarian when I failed to make smart decisions. My coaches identified this early on, and certainly used it to their advantage when I was too far gone.

Concerned that I needed assistance in my courses, my coaching staff arranged for me to meet with a tutor to help me with a required research paper due in a World Religion course. Soon, both the tutor and my coaching staff realized that I did not need assistance with anything regarding my classes. I simply refused to do the work because it was not important to me. I was able to pull my D up to a C, and I managed to pass one of my failing courses. Therefore, I was eligible for the rest of my freshman season. Threatening basketball was the sole reason I locked in on my work in finishing the semester—never mind the fact that in three main courses, I failed one and received below average grades in the other two. I could still play basketball, and that was all that mattered. My mother and coaches were content with me remaining eligible, but were equally frustrated that I'd waited until I was on the brink of disaster to put forth the proper effort and use my intellect.

As a result, my coaches tightened my academic restrictions in the spring semester. While the entire team was allowed three absences in their classes, I was granted one. My progress reports were weekly, and I had mandatory study hall three times a week with a member of our coaching staff. As a college freshman, being micromanaged like a child should have been embarrassing. My teammates cracking jokes about my academic standing should have been troubling, but it was not. Frankly, emerging as the face of Limestone Women's Basketball was enough.

Weeks into the spring semester, we began playing our conference schedule. Each game was an important one, with implications of where you were going to be seeded in the conference tournament and possibly earn an NCAA bid. Being that the core of our team was freshman and sophomores, we were still trying to establish who we were as a unit. We lacked cohesiveness, which made each game a challenge even when we played inferior opponents. Through our lack of chemistry, I averaged twenty points per game over our first five conference contests. I started to notice a shift in how I was received on campus. I was stopped by individuals who'd never seen me before, heaping buckets of praise and admiration over my head.

"Awesome game Shiloh!"

"I haven't seen a player like you since I have been here."

"There's the female Kobe!"

"Superstar, what's up?"

"Can you sign this program for me?"

Are you are asking ME for an autograph?

As much as I tried to reject these compliments, I began to embrace them and believed my own hype. I stopped deflecting the applause and began to internalize it. This was my first mistake, because I had now anchored my identity in the praise of others. This was the first step in setting myself up for failure. Too much of my worthiness was intertwined with the success of this game, and it was pushing me further from reality.

After some early success, I ran into the obstacles my coach warned me about the day he named me a starter. I produced single-digit scoring in three consecutive games and was having a tough time bringing myself out of this slump. Each game I came in confident, but if I did not get going offensively minutes into the game, I got down on myself, chalking it up to another terrible outing. This was the first time I felt my head coach was truly disappointed in me. Not because I was in the midst of a shooting slump, but because he saw me sliding back into the timid freshman that initially arrived on campus, simply because things were not going the way I intended.

During a practice in this stretch of games, I committed three turnovers in a row during an inter-squad scrimmage. My head coach slung his clipboard into the bleachers and screamed, "When are you going to grow up and stop acting like a baby?!" The brilliance of my head coach was his ability to understand what he needed to say or do to maximize our potential. He took the time to connect with us first as individuals. He learned what my triggers were and distinguished my ability to respond to him after he pushed me to the point of infuriation. He knew that making me angry would guide me out of this slump... and it did. I never took his words personally because of the bond we'd developed. He became a father figure in my life, and I appreciated that more than I could ever express to him.

After this particular practice, I was back to Shiloh. The rest of my games, I scored in the upper teens with a few twenty-point performances thrown into the mix. As a team, we are able to secure some pivotal wins, concluding the regular season as the number three seed going into a home match-up versus number six seed Belmont Abbey in the opening round of the conference tournament. Heading into the game, I slipped into the mindset of "one and we done," so I would not forget the magnitude of this moment. I was essentially given the greenlight by my coach, and I surfaced as our team's leading scorer. I was viewed as a big-time player with big-time talent, and with this being the biggest game of my short career, I was expected to lead us to new heights.

A day before the tournament was scheduled to start, Conference Carolinas individual awards were announced. I was named Conference Carolinas Freshman of the Year, the first in Limestone Women's basketball history and Second Team All-Conference Carolinas. When my coach informed me that I'd received these awards, I was elated thinking about how far I had come in six months. I was now achieving things I did not see as attainable before. I thought about how proud my tribe would be and how I put together one of the best seasons a freshman has ever had. My coach was proud of me, but he was not satisfied. He was sure to let me know that he was happy I was not named First Team All- Conference because that would give me something to strive towards in the following season. He always had a way of keeping things in perspective and wanting more from me. Besides, my season was not over yet.

1st Post Season Colligate Game
Belmont Abbey Vs Limestone College
March, 1st, 2010

Unlike the season opener, I woke up on this particular morning calm and relaxed. I wasn't at all concerned that I'd just missed my 9am class to get extra sleep to ensure that I'd be ready for tonight's game. I would deal with the consequences of that later. It was tournament time, and anything else was insignificant. I went through my normal pre-game routine, and by tip-off I was locked in, ready to seize the moment, and lead my team to victory. My jump shot was off early as I rushed some open looks and took questionable ones, being overly eager to come up big for my team. My coach pulled me aside for a minute to calm me down and get me settled into the rhythm of the game.

Belmont Abbey was not very talented, but they were tough, gritty, and made you work for every opportunity you wanted. We found ourselves in a battle early, but once I became infused in the flow of the game, I began to show why I was the team's best player all year. I put pressure on Belmont's defense as I quit settling for jump shots and attacked the rim, forcing their team to focus on me which presented opportunities for my teammates to score. But, as a unit, we were still out of sync. We struggled collectively and allowed Belmont Abbey to gain confidence as the game went on. This game was a mirror of what we had been all season, inconsistent. We fell to Belmont Abbey in my first post season game by eight points. I finished the match up with twenty-two points and was greeted with compliments by my tribe, fans, and a few opponents. I appreciated the love, but part of me knew that I did not do enough to lead my team to a win.

I concluded my freshman season averaging fifteen points per game and the best player on a very talented team. This fact brought a sense of contentment, not satisfaction. With the season ending, it gave me an opportunity to be better in my classes. I tried to convince myself that I would approach my school work in the same manner as basketball, but it did not work. I still missed classes and assignments, I was punished for violating team rules, and I was still micromanaged like a child. I finished the spring semester slightly improved from the first, but it was not because I studied hard or dedicated myself to my studies. It was because I carried a hidden intellect that glistens whenever I decide to display it, and some of my spring semester classes would not challenge a middle schooler. As a result of a poor fall semester, I was still at risk for ineligibility for my sophomore season, after failing a course and barely skating by in the others. So, I was placed in and accepted, elementary classes such as aerobic conditioning and flag football. None of which would equip me for a bright and productive future, but each would directly contribute to assuring my eligibility.

At this moment, I conceived that individuals, generally speaking, could and would make the road I traveled a lot easier, to the point that I could barely do enough and still get by.

Had I been concerned with anything other than basketball, I would not have put myself in this position. I would have recognized what people subconsciously thought about me and why this route was presented to me as an option. To them, I was just another black athlete who devalued education, but excelled athletically. Yes, it was insulting and disrespectful for them to assume, but my reader, you must understand that I gave them a reason to do so. As Dean Davenport of Hillman College reminded me, "It's bad enough when others disrespect our people, but it's doubly offensive when we do it to ourselves."

By the end of my freshman year, I grew as a basketball player, but not as a student or a person. The majority of my teammates had stellar academic years and were prepared to start taking courses within their major the following year. Most of them cultivated meaningful friendships outside of basketball and were slowly growing into young women. I, on the other hand, remained the same hollow, immature, introverted freshman that arrived on campus in August. Yes, a multitude of students and faculty knew of me and about me, but no one truly knew me. I did not allow anyone to experience Maria—only Shiloh.

Before I returned home for the summer, I was required to meet with my coach for our exit meeting. The purpose of this meeting was to inform me of what I did well during my freshman season and what areas needed improvement—my defense, mid-range game, overall conditioning, and shooting. Coach was sure to reiterate how the summer was a critical time to work on my individual game outside of the team and how most players made the biggest jump of improvement from their freshman to sophomore year. It was no misunderstanding on how critical this summer was going to be for me. Next season, I would be the focal point of every opponents scouting report. Their main goal would be to stop #24. It was time to elevate to the next level. Challenge accepted.

5

Kinships

Immediately following our conference tournament loss, Coach held an awards meeting where the team could vote on our individual awards with the MVP and the Pride, Hustle, and Desire awards to be distributed at our school wide awards banquet. The Defensive Player of the Year Award was to be given amongst the team at our annual team dinner. When the time came, I was excited about attending my first awards banquet, but I was equally nervous thinking about walking across the stage in front of the entire school. I was very confident that I was going to receive the MVP award simply based on everything I'd accomplished over the season. In my mind, I was the most valuable piece to our team, and I had the stats to prove it.

When it is time for our team to be presented with our awards, the school's Athletic Director took a few minutes to speak about some of our defining moments throughout the season and some outstanding individual performances. This produced a gratifying feeling when my name was mentioned on several occasions during his speech. He proceeded to present our starting point guard with the Pride, Hustle, and Desire award. It was safe to assume that this was a unanimous decision as she was leadership personified on and off the court. At last, it was time for the MVP award to be handed out. Coach went into his soliloquy about what the most valuable player stood for and what it said about the individual who receives it—as decided by fellow teammates.

When Coach announced the name of the winner, it was not my name he relayed. I discreetly slipped down in my chair, embarrassed as I hoped no one saw me begin to rise. I was deflated and disappointed, not in my teammate's accomplishment, but disappointed in how this moment solidified where I thought I was in my friendships with some of my teammates. I honestly believed that, no matter what issues arose off the court, there was no way you could not respect me as a basketball player. But, I was wrong. I felt I was denied an award that was rightfully mine. The kinship I once shared with every one of my teammates had now been altered as I began to look at some of them with questioning eyes, a far cry from our introductory period.

The day I arrived on campus, the connection I formed with my teammates was instantaneous. These were the ladies that carried a similar love of basketball, and for the next six to seven months, I was going to be spending more time with them than my blood family. There were five additional freshmen who committed to Limestone when I did, and from the very beginning, we knew that we could create something special that would attach us forever. Calling ourselves the "Freshman Crew," each one of us was uniquely gifted in talent and personality, creating an interesting balance on and off the court.   Crew member number one, was one of the greatest individuals you could ever meet, and yes, she was that way at eighteen. There was literally nothing she could not do between the lines of ninety-four feet of basketball court. Her prominence was displayed through her studies as well. She was the prototype of what a student athlete is supposed to be—everything I was not. Crew member two, was a direct and tough person who's previous friendship made my transition into college easier. Her strong personality was a gift and a curse in our friendship, but even when we were not in agreeance she always had my back. Crew member three, was the joy and exhilaration of our team. She had a way of being able to make a bad day good and a good day even better—always hilarious and forever keeping circumstances loose and entertaining. Crew member four, was a sparkplug who never withheld her energy or encouragement. I refer to her as 'the glue' because of the exclusive connections she had with each one of us. Finally, crew member five, the individual I had the deepest connection with and the person who understood me on a level that no one could. Our similarities were evident both on and off the court. She remains one of my closest friends to this day.

Although the Freshman Crew constructed an impenetrable bond, it spilled over onto our other teammates as well, including the seniors. I united with a particular senior who took it upon herself to take me under her wing and assist me through some of my early struggles at Limestone. During the preseason, the Freshman Crew and a few of our seniors went to a local restaurant named "The Clock." We sat there for hours, conversing over a wide range of topics. Everything from our families, to our high school experiences, music, movies, relationship problems, and how we were adjusting to Limestone. We shared our stories and exchanged infinite laughs, making the evening blissful and forming a kinship where our friendships were molded into family connections. I was extremely thankful to come into a situation that developed into a family atmosphere.

I could tell that my odd sense of humor was beginning to rub off on them. Prior to my arrival, my childhood friends and I developed our own, weird but playful dialect. We would add extra Z's and S's to certain words when we spoke. For example, when relaying a message of, "I have to get up early in the morning," we would say, "I gots to wake up wits the birds in za morning!" Strange, I know, but this is how we entertained ourselves. Once I became comfortable around my teammates, I began to speak with them in this dialect. Some simply laughed, but others began to use it as well. It was light-hearted fun, which was what we were all about. Including countless nights of freestyling over the hottest beats and harmonizing the most recent records, making every day lively.

From that point on, we did everything together. We went out to the movies, bowling, shopping, eating, walking to classes, and relaxing together after solid workouts. Our team became inseparable, and if you had a problem with one of us, you were going to have to deal with all of us. One night, our entire team was close to getting in a physical altercation on campus with, let's say, a few dozen locals. At the time, there was a YMCA branch located directly across the sidewalk from our gymnasium. A couple of us were exiting the gym, and a local high school student tried to charm one of my teammates. When she rejected his offer, he called her a very unflattering name. An argument ensued and the high school student called his relatives to come to the campus to "deal" with my teammate. In return, we called the rest of our teammates to come to the parking lot as we are not going to allow our sister to be harmed by anyone.

When two car loads of Gaffney locals pulled up, people started pouring out of each car. One had a baby on her hip, and another woman was screaming, yelling, putting phones down and taking earrings off. We quickly figured out that she was the sister of the high school student. The entire situation began to amuse us, which aggravated the locals, resulting in more arguments as the words become more vicious. As the situation continued to escalate, a few of our teammates called additional friends as reinforcement. I looked to my left and my right to see where my teammates were and which people were beside me.

As I was scanning the crowd, I saw faint movement behind a tree. It startled me at first, so I discreetly leaned and ducked behind a person beside me to better observe who was behind the tree. As my vison cleared, I realized that it was one of my teammates who was terrified about the situation. Her body jerked in the opposite direction each time a local glanced her way. Laughter ensued when I pointed her out to the rest of team. We respected the fact that she wasn't "bout that life." The hostility only subdued when other students and athletes showed up and the locals realized they were supremely outnumbered. We chuckled and conversed for hours, in disbelief of what had just happened. But, it was well understood that we were always going to be there one another, no matter how foolish or outrageous the situation was.

One of my fondest memories was our movie nights in our senior's dorm room. Each week, we came together and picked a movie to watch. This specific night, the group decided to watch "Twilight." At that time, I was unfamiliar with this film and the books because the concept seemed very bizarre to me. I did not tell them until years later that I fell in love with the movie and became quite a Robert Pattison fanatic. As silly as that may seem, the significance is, by associating with these individuals I was being exposed to different ideas and interests that I would never have considered prior to meeting them.

We were experiencing all that college had to offer, including the night life. Almost every weekend, we attended any and every party we were invited to or heard about. We were often the life of these functions, singing and dancing into the wee hours, never concerned about tomorrow. We were creating memories that would last a lifetime. We shared countless Thursday nights in a place called "Smitty's"—a hole in the wall establishment close to campus that reminded me of home. The majority of the African American students on campus frequented this spot each week to feel of sense of unity. Smitty's was uncomfortably hot, with the blanketed smell of Black and Mild smoke and fish grease from the dinners sold out back, but that was what made it ours. Each week, the DJ played the hottest records released and we would execute the latest dances to go along with them. The magnitude of these moments is almost indescribable as each of my teammates holds a prominent place in my life.

My happiest memory of my team was New Year's Eve 2009. Our entire team, including a specific member who NEVER went out, we slayed up in our best outfits as we had plans to bring in the New Year at a club in Greenville, South Carolina. Excitement built as we traveled the highway, blasting music and singing at the top of our lungs. We arrived in the parking lot of the club only to see that this establishment had been closed, as in shut down; as in, boards on the windows shut down. We then decided to go to a familiar club in Spartanburg, South Carolina to celebrate the night instead. We were in our cars when the clock struck midnight. We laughed hysterically and screamed, "HAPPY NEW YEAR" to each other. It did not matter that our plans were obliterated and that we spent part of our New Year's celebration in a car instead of on a dance floor. We had each other and that was all that mattered.

Further into my freshman year, as my "Shiloh" persona grew and other members of the freshman crew continued to forge their own path athletically, some bonds began to shift. The type of success and recognition I had led me to presenting myself as someone larger than life. This created a rift with some of our upperclassman who thought I received special treatment from my coaching staff. This created jealousy of my former and current success. A specific kinship with a senior took a major hit during this time. Soon after my coach named me as starter, this senior and I had an in-depth conversation about what transpired. I was reassured that there were no ill feelings towards me. Part of me accepted that as fact, but part me did not cave into being naïve. She was the star before I came to Limestone and an ultra-competitor. Initially, she may have been genuinely happy for me when she thought I was going to exist in her shadow, but I do not believe she felt I would ever surpass her in her senior season. Becoming who I was, being insensitive to her situation, AND seeing me transcend in her position was not an easy circumstance to accept. As the season progressed, we did not spend as much time together, we did not speak on a regular basis, and there was a constant underlying tension between the two of us.

I became bitter because I desired the kinship we had prior to the discord, but I felt like the love was no longer authentic and that I was disliked over something I could not control. For a mature being, a conversation should have been initiated and a solution should have been sought, because this was family. I allowed my bitterness to turn me into someone who was disingenuous and untrustworthy. I created scenarios and circumstances that continued to shatter the bond we once had. The introvert in me craved being seen in a favorable and sympathetic light, and I tried to achieve that by being vocal about my ill feelings toward her. Though there were transgressions by both parties, the conflict became heightened in my entitled self-absorbency.

Additionally, I believe the freshman crew attitude that we established irritated some of the team, as remarks about us thinking we were the whole team were guised as jokes. But most joking matters contain undertones of true feelings. One person began to see how establishing a "crew" within a team could further divide us, as she had a crystal vision of the larger picture. Internally, our discord grew has different upperclassmen had their own separate issues with various members of the freshman crew, and we naturally aligned ourselves with each other.

Despite all the tension, when it was time for the banquet, not earning the MVP award never entered my mind, because despite internal turmoil, basketball remained the common ground. I had been the best player all season, but I was not well-liked or respected by some because I was not the best teammate. That is the ultimate reason the MVP award went to another team member. It had nothing to do with my stats, and everything to do with my character, or lack thereof. As a twenty-six-year-old woman, I accept the divisiveness of my actions and demeanor. As a nineteen-year-old child, this felt like betrayal.

The night after the banquet, some of the team attended a small get together at one of the houses we frequented throughout the season. I was physically present, but mentally, I was still struggling to process what transpired. I began to think about each of my teammates and wondered if they voted for me. I knew which ones would not, but the troublesome part were the ones I wasn't sure about. I instantly told myself that, while I had love for my teammates, my guard would remain up with most of them.

The banquet experience and coaches' exit meeting set the tone for the type of summer I was going to have. When I returned home for the summer, I allowed myself two weeks to catch up with high school friends and family before I began my summer regimen. I ate, drank, and slept basketball. I worked out six days a week, alone, no rebounder, no workout partners, and no trainers. I created my own skill development and conditioning workouts based off material my coaches extended to me. I purposely worked out in gyms with no air conditioning and used every negative experience from my freshman year as motivation. I did not converse with many of my teammates over the summer, as I was determined that no one was going to outwork me. I became so focused on basketball, I no longer concerned myself with what people thought about me. I invested everything into basketball, and anything outside of that had little-to-no value in my life. I gave the game my soul and sacrificed Maria for the glory of Shiloh. My goal was to return my sophomore year in the best shape of my career, ready to have the best year in my short span, leaving no doubt about who the best really was.

6

Canonize

Returning to Limestone my second year, one thing was evident, the change in my demeanor was visible. Though pre-season was about polishing our individual skill set heading into the season, we were still competing with our teammates, pushing one another to be the best we could be. The keyword in the last sentence is "with." I was not competing with my team; I was competing against them. I was egotistical and my arrogance grew each day, even though it was rooted in masking my actual feelings. I harbored a nonchalant attitude and carried a sense of invincibility fused with entitlement. I could do and say anything because of who I was and because of my athletic skills. Seldom was there a place I traveled where a student, city resident, or child did not tell me how much they enjoyed watching me play and the excitement I brought to their city. Every restaurant, mall, or gas station I stepped into showered me with undeniable flattery. So much of it went directly to the pedestal I stood on, and I lost a very important trait my tribe instilled in me: humility.

My response to every word of praise was, "Thank you," but internally I was thinking, "I know how good I am, but it's nice that you notice." My coaches began to take note of my superior attitude as well. Although the team still had our core nucleus together, and added a suburb juco forward, our vocal leadership graduated with the senior class the previous season. My coaches needed me to step up and fill the gap left behind. Countless meetings were held about my leadership capabilities. The coaching staff had a way of seeing the best in me when I could not see it in myself. The more I thought about their request, the more I knew I was the wrong person for the job. Leadership meant having the ability to encourage everyone to believe in the vision and aspirations of the program. Your leader must have the skill of stepping up and unifying the group when hardships fall upon you. A leader has the responsibility of uplifting and motivating every person on the team, from the starters to the last player on the bench. How could I lead when I did not truly know some of my teammates because I never initiated spending any time with them? I never took the time to discover their strengths and weaknesses, therefore I could not develop a tactic to encourage them when the time permitted.

I knew I couldn't lead when I was a part of what divided us. I could not offer clarity and courage when I had not developed those qualities in myself. You could rely on me to rise to the occasion between the lines, but inspiring a teammate to believe that their highest goal is achievable, I would fall short every single time. The most important quality of a leader is leading by example, but in order to lead by example, you must first BE an example. On the basketball court, I could be an example. I worked hard, I was very skilled, dominant, and there was not much of anything I could not do within those ninety-four feet. However, an authentic leader of example commands multiple aspects of their life and provokes others to strive to be their best. A leader does not nearly exceed classroom absences only a month into the school year, nor do they attend a campus party knowing assignments are due and studying needs to commence. What leadership example is shackled by pride, or refuses to ask for assistance in classes you find challenging, so you walk out early or listen to music when it is time to take notes? A leader is not weak enough to allow themselves to exist in marginalized boxes and internalize other people's low expectations for their life.

I could not be an example for anyone else when I could not be an example to myself first. I appreciated my coaching staff for the depth of their belief and for seeing gold underneath the armor of conceit, but I knew this responsibility was something I would not be able to carry. I accepted who I had become.

At the jumpstart of the season, our team got off to a very inconsistent start: win one, lose two, win two, and lose three. A contributing factor was our starting point guard, now a junior, missing a handful of games because of a shoulder injury. I was switched to point guard during her absence which did wonders for my personal game, but it came at the detriment of the team. Our point guard was the floor general, a traditional point guard who served as an extension of the coach. I, on the other hand, was a green-lit bonafide scorer. I was not a point guard, let alone a pass first point guard. I was option one. If option one was not available on most occasions, that was the only time the ball moved. My style of play contributed to the larger chemistry issue our team had. If we were not in transition, we struggled immensely offensively. We lacked ball movement, spacing, and cohesiveness. Oddly enough, individually I flourished amongst the chaos on the court, averaging almost twenty points per game and leading the entire conference in scoring as a sophomore. Remember, my goal for this year was to be the best player Limestone College had seen up until that point.

I want to refer to the word 'cohesiveness' for a moment. Cohesiveness means: the quality of forming a united whole. We certainly were not united. Our team was a team of clicks. We held conversations in relation to basketball, but outside of Timken gymnasium, certain players only hung out with certain players and vice versa. I was rarely seen with anyone outside of my selection of three teammates I felt I could trust. If you are wondering, yes, the Freshman Crew broke off into separate factions. The deficiency of harmony did not stop at teammates, as some of us were not at peace with members of our coaching staff. As the season, progressed my relationship with my head coach was becoming complex. The previous season, I clung to his every word and harbored a fresh sense of invincibility each time he encouraged me. This season was slightly different, as I began to feel that Coach was doing more to make sure I knew I was not better than the group. His constant remarks about the faces I made while I was playing began to annoy me, and I viewed it as him nit-picking over things that really did not matter. When I took a bad shot, his words shifted from, "You can get a better shot than that" to, "This is not the Limestone Maria's." I got called out in front of my team more than I liked and I felt singled out at times.

In an early conference match-up against Queens University, I got into a verbal altercation with a teammate in the middle of the game. It escalated to the point that we almost needed to be separated. I was the first person my coach screamed at. Subconsciously, I was thinking, *"Why is this man yelling at me like I am the only person who did something wrong?"* Coach and I exchanged some unpleasantries, and he threatened to send me to the locker room, but opted for benching me the entire half. We ended up losing the game by double digits, because mentally, we were not able to recover from these altercations combined with poor play.

Our very next practice was brutal and Coach made the entire team, except me and the individual I argued with run. Ultimately, I felt awful for the team paying for my poor decision. My anger towards my head coach was visible. At the time, I received this as my coach attempting to keep me in my place and reducing what I meant to the program, rather than him trying to illustrate how divisive my actions had become. The staff and I had several verbal exchanges, with one escalating to the point I where was prepared to be suspended or sent home. The complexity lied in the aftermath of these disagreements. We would calm down, talk things over, and all was right with the world until the same thing happened weeks later. Our lack of togetherness, from the top to the bottom, as a unit directly contributed to our erratic play. We simply were not in sync on or off the basketball court.

Slightly passed the halfway mark in the season, we are informed that our home game versus Mt. Olive (one of the best teams in the conference) was selected to be nationally broadcasted on CBS College Sports, the first in Limestone Women's basketball history. I scanned to my left and right, seeing my teammates flash the same Kool-Aid smile I had injected a new sense of excitement into us. I left that meeting and called my mother, telling her how ecstatic I was, but also worried. We had lost four of our last six games, our chemistry showed no signs of improving, we had infighting with teammates and coaches disagreements, and our overall team morale was pretty low. Despite all our issues, I prayed this opportunity would provide the spark we needed to turn our season around.

JANUARY 29th, 2011
Mt. Olive College vs Limestone College
TV: CBS College Sports

I tried to approach this game like it was simply another regular season game, not only to keep routine, but to also keep my nerves at bay. There were a lot of questions surrounding this game. Would we step up and beat the second-best team in the conference? Would our infighting continue to be our Achilles heel? Would the bright lights of the national TV spotlight overwhelm us? And lastly, would Coach's lineup change be the type of shake up we needed? After our team prayer, before we took the floor for warm-ups, I felt an intense yet calming presence come over me, as if God was saying, "Let go and leave your worries in my hands."

A line from one of my favorite songs repeatedly echoed in my head: "This is my moment. I've waited all my life. I can tell it's time." I examined my teammates and their faces. I had never seen us more focused then we are in this moment. As the starters took the floor before tip-off, I was joined by our normal starting point guard, who had recovered from her injury, two additional Freshman Crew members who were also guards and one post player. The blueprint of Limestone Women's basketball's—four guards around one post player—dribble- drive motion offense was born. This offense was the final solution to all our problems on the basketball court. Our offensive fire power created match-up nightmares for Mt. Olive as we surrounded our post player with four guards who could hit the open three, create their own shot, and facilitate plays for others. The electricity felt within this game was a feeling that remains stitched in my being. We had finally arrived.

This line-up opened the entire floor for me and my teammates, which provided us with the necessary space to play more freely. With a number of mismatches that favored our team, Mt. Olive had a tough time defending us man-to-man, so they would periodically switch to a match-up zone that did not assist them in their struggles. Our three-point shooters were able to find the holes within the defense and receive open shots. In our time playing with one another, I do not remember an instance when we fused together so seamlessly. Every one of us felt it during the course of this game. We looked at each other and saw the same reassurance we felt internally, and it was beautiful.

With Mt. Olive being the second-best team in the conference, they did not go out without a fight. Down the stretch, we made some careless turnovers that gave them momentum to get back in the game. Cutting the lead to single digits with under two minutes of play, my closest friend and the spark plug of the team blew passed one defender and crossed another, getting into the teeth of their zone, forcing the bottom girl to step up into help side, which left me wide open in the corner. With time clicking off the shot clock I nail the biggest three of my career, facilitated by my teammate. We went on to close the game out, beating Mt. Olive seventy-four to sixty-eight. I finished with a game high twenty-three points.

Inside our locker room, you could sense that this moment was indeed the turning point I'd prayed it would be. Not only had we just made history, we discovered a system that no opponent had an answer for, and it fit all of our individual games like a glove. We also showed ourselves how great we could be, and what we could achieve when we abandoned our differences. Our team, school, communities, and families came together to make that day unforgettable. I do not think we had a true understanding of the power we had over so many people collectively.

My family opted to gather at my grandmother's home in Shiloh for a community watch party. My mother drove from Asheville immediately after the game to pick me up and bring me home for the night so I could see how many people were rooting for me. As we pulled up to my grandmother's home, the street was lined with cars. My uncles, in the crisp January mountain air, were cooking on the grill and all of my tribe were waiting for my arrival. I entered the house to a round of applause, laughter, and plenty of hugs from everyone. The amount of love I received this day from my team, coaches, and peers was overwhelming, and despite the conflict, I was incredibly grateful to have shared this experience with them.

We went on to win eleven of our last thirteen games, including a huge road win over top-seeded Barton College on their senior and church night. We edged a tenacious Erskine College team in the first round of the conference tournament, making up for our early exit in the previous season and my quiet play in crunch time of that game. I scored thirty points in our opening round, making sure I did not make the same mistake as the previous year. Our semi-final game presented us with a rematch against Mt. Olive. Since they were the higher seed, we had to play them on the road. It was a back and forth battle throughout the game, and their veteran players made big plays down when needed. We fell in this semi-final game, but unlike the previous year, there was a lot of optimism surrounding us. We made tremendous strides as a young group, and each year we were getting closer to a championship. Our issues were dropped at the gym door as we realized basketball was the sanctuary.

As a sophomore, I assembled one of the best seasons

in Limestone Women's Basketball history, averaging twenty points per game. I was named the Conference Carolina Scoring Champion, First Team All-Conference, and was a mere fifty-five points away from being a one-thousand-point scorer. I indeed achieved my goal of leaving no doubt that I was the best player on my team. Academically, I remained consistently low in attendance and my overall performance. Being that the majority of my classes were sports based, I could skip a few days and remain afloat, because I did well on the tests. School was something I had to do to remain eligible. I did not view my education as a pathway to endless opportunities. Everything revolved around basketball. Assignments were turned in late, even after I had clear knowledge that points would be deducted. If I was tired from a game or practice, I missed classes to chill or relax to prepare myself for the next on-court encounter. Tests or quizzes were made up at a later date if I explained why I wanted to postpone taking it with the rest of the class. I produced the bare minimum out of sheer laziness and low expectation.

Concluding this school year, I reached new heights athletically and saw potential to grasp every accolade I'd dreamed of as a child. I was flying and standing atop my pedestal at its highest peak; nothing could cut me down. You would think, for an athlete of my popularity and stature, that I would be surrounded by countless people and desolation would be foreign. For me, my phone barely rung and knocks seldom found my door. At the peak of my success, I was as reclusive as I had ever been.

SINGULAR

Existing in the depth of seclusion

Though blessings rain down, I'm steadily losing

Peace of mind?

A fleeting illusion

Desperately longing to be received in this world so cold

While conserving the sweetest parts of my soul

Young, black, athletic wiz

Special combo

The irony is......

That's why I'm alone.

7

Kinships Part 2

Traditionally, I have always been a slight loner. I find comfort in being able to sit with my thoughts and feelings by myself, but this comfort is often rooted in self-doubt. As a twenty-year-old college student, my interests could be viewed as singular, and I was not prepared to stand in that truth. I loved watching classic black sitcoms such as Good Times, Sanford and Son, and What's Happening, but my favorites were A Different World and Martin. There were days that I would lock myself in my room and watch reruns of Martin and A Different World, not only because they were classics, but because I had ample time to fantasize about having those types of friendships, existing in a place where every person around me could be considered a sister or a brother. I carried this bond with my childhood tribe, and although we spoke often, we were spread around different colleges and universities throughout the southeast, living our own lives.

With my childhood tribe, I never had to question

if they were authentic or sincere. They knew who I was, my likes, dislikes, strengths and flaws, and loved me for them. You will never hear me refer to my childhood tribe as "friends," as the term does not sufficiently describe the depth of our relationships. A huge part of me yearned for that comradery with my teammates, especially all the ladies I came in with. The one trait I possessed, that could be a gift and a curse, was my stubbornness. On one hand, it allowed me to fight for my beliefs, but on the other, it shackled me to never being willing to compromise, even when it could be beneficial for me to do so. In this case, it was a curse.

Early on in my career, I tried to approach my team with an open heart and mind, but after a significant time of internal conflict, arguments, and unflattering words shared to my face and behind my back, I had almost completely shut down. Instead of speaking directly with these individuals, I felt hurt or misunderstood. My stubbornness allowed me to shrug it off and fold inward. I internally minimized my communication and held grudges against people whom I'd deemed untrustworthy. Immaturity and my unshakeable thoughts, let small conflicts devalue meaningful friendships.

I believe that a lot of problems we had within our team was the disparity in personal growth. Our upperclassman had developed from eighteen year-old kids to twenty-one and twenty-two-year old young adults. They understood in a year or two that they were going to integrate themselves into their professional careers someday soon. Our upperclassman prepared themselves for what came next. That meant not attending every campus event, kickback, or party because they had a clear understanding of the larger picture. They ceased living for the moment, and several underclassmen began adapting to this ideology, finding a healthy balance of recreation and studies. Leadership within our team reached out to me on several occasions, attempting to expose me to a different way of thinking, but what could you tell a twenty-year old sophomore with mounds of adoration at her feet, and who could do and say anything to receive what she wanted? Not. A. Word.

After a while, I grew tired of being lectured, and instead of receiving the advice, I began to verbalize my displeasure with people for telling me how to live my life. If it did not affect my production on the basketball court, what was my incentive to alter my way of living? This was the type of mindset you adapt when your entire life is wrapped up in a sport. The sport becomes the base of your existence.

Our conflict came to a head near the end of the regular season, which fractured my relationship with a few teammates for years to come. It was a typical Saturday night on campus. A few teammates and I were relaxing when we get got invited to a house party off campus. I retreat to my room to prepare for the night and a few members of my team were there upon my arrival. No words were exchanged. I just bypassed them and got dressed. Approximately thirty minutes later, a teammate I was attending the party with entered my room with an alcoholic beverage, alerting me that she was ready to go. I reached into my freezer to retrieve my own alcohol, bypassing my teammates once more, and left for the party. When we got to the house, everyone was excited to see us. We headed to the dance floor for another night of blissful fun.

Shortly after we got on the dance floor, a teammate notified me that a few of our other team members back at the dorms told our head coach we violated the team's forty-eight-hour rule. The forty-eight-hour rule stated that no player could consume alcohol forty-eight hours prior to a game. We were to be in action the following Monday. My teammate looked around, as we had a very good idea of who the snitches could be. There were no words to describe the amount of anger and rage that struck my body. We left the party abruptly, and during the car ride back to the dorm, I accepted the fact that I was about to get into a physical altercation with some of my teammates, and I was prepared for the consequences that came along with it. When we arrived at the dorm, I stormed up the three flights of stairs. No one was in the room when I got there. I searched the hallways and other rooms belonging to my teammates, but again, I found no one.

At practice the following afternoon, I entered the gym and the locker room completely silent out of fear of what I would say or do if provoked. I got dressed and sat on the furthest bleacher from my entire team as we waited for the guys' team to finish their practice. I was emotionally drained. It pained me that some of my teammates would go to such lengths to disrupt my career and all I tried to accomplish. I shared countless unforgettable memories with these individuals no longer than a year ago, and now they were the cause of this pain. People I would have gone to war for, I was now at war with. It broke me to feel like physically taking my frustration out on family. I sat in silence with my outrage, thankful that we were about to practice so I could funnel my feelings into the game.

Ironically, we had one of the best practices of the season that day. This was a fascinating aspect about my team. Off the court, we could be separate, not talking to one another, and having problems, but none of that was evident when we stepped on the court. We cheered each other on, extended congratulatory hand claps and fist pumps, and most importantly, we had one another's back. At different points throughout the practice, I could see all eyes were on me, waiting to see if my anger would cease. As much as I loved the way we were playing, that was all it was. Basketball was our untouchable sanctuary because we all wanted the best for the program. But, for some of my teammates, that was where the love stopped.

When practice was over, the teammate who attended the party with me and I were called into a meeting with our head coach. He asked us about the accuracy of the accusations brought to his attention. We went on to explain that no rules were broken because we did not drink any alcohol. Before you wonder, no it was not a lie. We were not at the party long enough to sip anything. Coach did not fault us for being college students, for going to a party, but he let his displeasure be known about our poor decision making. By the grace of God, we were not suspended or disciplined for this incident. Unfortunately, the damage was already done. I accepted that I had to treat certain teammates like complete strangers, essentially censoring all my words and actions around them. I hated this reality, but I had no choice but to live in it.

Our coaching staff called a team meeting shortly after this incident, in hopes of mending some of our brokenness. Everyone was given the opportunity to express their concerns and feelings. Individuals spoke about our team being separated and how it felt to be left out or made to feel differently because they were not a part of an inner circle. People became emotional when speaking about other players and the conflicts they had with one another. Then, there was me. I sat quietly, observing everyone, feeling the sincerity in some and questioning it in others. I did not speak until my coach pointed at me and said, "You have not said what you need to say." I pondered his words for a moment, having an internal tug of war. Part of me wanted to be vulnerable and say how I felt, in hopes of rebuilding these friendships, but other parts of me wanted to stay angry and reserved, keeping my pins close to my chest.

My stubbornness prevailed, and choking down tears, I said, "I have a lot going on, and sometimes I don't even want to be here." Unbeknownst to a large part of my team, throughout the season, I had suffered personal turmoil, almost losing an uncle to a brain aneurysm and the death of my grandfather only months later. I only shared the news with my coaching staff and my closest friends, attempting to sort through my pain in my own way—meaning I put all my emotions into basketball. The sentence above is the sole statement I made in this meeting. Though I do not place sole blame for our dissention on my shoulders, I failed to use my importance to ameliorate our disputes. This meeting was my chance to show my teammates that I could meet them at their vulnerability by sharing personal tragedy and being able to articulate my frustration with them in a respectable way, with the objective of going back to the reason we became a family in the first place. My team was defenseless in this meeting, and I inflicted the same pain I harbored upon them after they laid their armor down. I was not ready to step into my accountability for the role I played in what divided us. The majority of the team gained clarity and insight into one another, while I left the meeting the same way I entered it, great with the few I trusted, and a barricade around my heart with the ones I didn't. My team accepted me for what I was, and I was not willing to do much of anything to change that.

I did not take interest in the group. The very love, loyalty, and respect I needed and expected, I was not willing to give. I chose to focus on what made us different rather than explore our similarities. Most importantly, I had not developed a skill that I could transform into a healthy conflict-resolution. My brass exterior helped me affirm that I did not need anyone or anything outside of the game of basketball, and my reputation was molded in that revelation. I became known as the young woman with tremendous talent, but a questionable attitude, lacking humility and social skills. My dear reader, the shameful thing about this was, I had no reasonable argument to rival this. Again, I leaned on basketball to keep my self-respect intact.

8

Three

Several changes had taken place entering my third year at Limestone. The first was a change in our coaching staff. One of my assistant coaches accepted a new job at a mid-major division 1 school, and I never accepted the coach who took his place. This new coach would never be able to understand me the way my exiting coach had. When my head coach and I would have our arguments, this particular coach would step in and guide me into seeing a different perspective, but he would never disregard my feelings as they were always valid to him. He also spoke about the potential he saw in me, revealing things I was too shallow to see in myself. Part of me never believed what he said, which is why he would reiterate, "You might not understand it now, but later you will." The day he called to tell me he had accepted a new position, I muffled my tears as he explained it was the best decision for him and his family. I never faulted him for making that choice, and I was disappointed that I did not express how much I appreciated him for his willingness to be more than a coach to me. He was tribe, and his presence in my everyday life was missed, immensely.

Secondly, I started to notice a change within my body. I played a lot of minutes in my sophomore year, and it took me nearly a month to resume working out once the season concluded. My recovery time after workouts and practices were a lot longer than before, and I was experiencing constant pain in my left knee. Our athletic training staff diagnosed me with Patella Tendonitis that could only be managed through everyday treatment, including game days. The pain was not severe, but it was nagging and forced me to alter some parts of my game. In my previous seasons, my ability to put the ball on the floor and get to the rim, in addition to my three-point and mid-range game, made me a very challenging guard. Due to this injury and the progression of my jump shot, I relied on my outside game a little more than I desired. This was the first time in my career that I could feel the game taking a toll on me physically. A hairline fracture in my right foot sidelined me for the last three weeks of pre-season. This was the first time I missed significant time away from basketball, and I was worried about how prepared I would be for the upcoming season. Every day, I went through a range of emotions. One minute I was optimistic that everything would work out fine, and the next minute, I was concerned about my productivity when I did return. I failed to concentrate on anything outside of my recovery. Again, this included my classwork.

During the fall semester of my junior year, my advisor forced me to take more core courses within my major of sports management, after I had avoided these courses my first two years. It is critical to understand that I chose sports management as my major at the time, because once my career ended, I knew I would still need sports in my life. Since I avoided taking these core courses, I placed myself in a position where I had to take some of my toughest classes all in the same semester. Managerial accounting was a foreign language to me, and I disliked the teaching techniques of my general biology and U.S history professors. Both wrote notes on the board with the expectation that the students would copy them all within the class time, without real direction. Someone like me, who lacked internal disciple and futuristic vision, was not successful in these courses. The absence of structure gave me too much leeway, and I was not responsible enough to be handed that type of freedom in a class.

By this time, my coaching staff came to terms with the fact that I was satisfied with the bare minimum, but that did not stop the occasional lectures. Young athletes, I need you to read these next sentences astutely. Every college coach is not like the head coach I played for. I was a junior at this point, which meant I was twenty-one years old. A lot of coaches would have given up on me and accepted that this was just who I was going to be, another great basketball player that refused to see that life had more meaning than temporary satisfaction. Some coaches would be fine with that fact, because you are still producing for them on the basketball court, baseball or football field. You are supposed to stand tall under both terms of being student athlete, and the NCAA stands firm in that message.

What they do not like to share is that these college and universities generate millions from their athletic programs— money generated off your hard work and skill. Some athletic departments can steer athletes into majors with virtually no job field, hiding behind the guise of making things easier for "you" in the moment, but in reality, it is so you remain eligible to preform, which directly benefits them. Individuals don't realize, or simply do not care, that this system is setting so many athletes up for failure. This was where being prepared and making choices anchored in that preparedness became a major factor. If you enter college informed, you have already broken a cycle of self-destruction because you are aware of the system you are inheriting. I was blessed with a coach that cared enough to try and illustrate the dangers of the path I took, but I was too audacious to receive his message.

October 1st, 2011 will forever be remembered as the day I began to slowly unravel. On this night, I received a phone call from a close friend. When I saw her name displayed on my phone, I became puzzled because she never called me so late. I was apprehensive about answering, but I pressed the receive button, in case it was an emergency. She asked if I had heard about what was going on back home, and I told her I had not. My friend told me there was a horrific car accident outside of an apartment complex a relative of hers resided in. Word was traveling around the city that the victim of this wreck was a childhood friend of mine. I tensed, as I felt agony begin to flow through my body, from the crown of my head to the bottom of my feet. I asked if she knew for sure it was him, and she said she didn't. I hung up with her in a quest to find out if the news was true. I pulled up Facebook, which was the equivalent to Newsweek, and saw several conflicting statuses about what happened to my friend. I realized my only option was to call his family. I hesitate, a piece of me didn't want to know the truth because it might shatter me into unrecognizable pieces you would mistake for a pillar of salt, but the agony of not knowing was equally painful. I could not bare to call his parents, to hear their tone of voice, so I opted to text one of his closest relatives.

From the moment I hit send, to the moment I received a reply, it was as if time stood still. I read the reply and it confirmed my fear, one of my best, childhood friends had been killed in a car accident. I stood in shock, not knowing what to do or say. I slowly placed my phone into my pocket and got a ride back to my dorm. When I arrived, I shut the door behind me and collapsed to the floor. I placed my forearm over my mouth to muffle my distress, laid on the ground, and cried. Tears blurred my vison as I drowned in my water, not only crying over the loss of my friend, but the pain, loneliness, and isolation manifested through it. I went into prayer. I turned to God for the strength to move forward through this intolerable grief. I took to social media in the early morning hours, pinned a tribute to my friend, and changed all my profile pictures to him. I used social media to verbalize the words I could not bring myself to say. I cried myself to sleep that night and found no relief in waking up the following morning.

I was grateful that a few of my teammates expressed concern and extended their condolences. I acknowledged their effort, but was in no state to further the conversation. I talked to my mother and my tribe as much as possible for comfort, updates, and my personal sanity. With the funeral being scheduled for later the following week, I had three days at Limestone before I could join my family. I did not attend any classes during this span, and still being sidelined with my foot injury, I was not able to participate in basketball activities. Since we were amid pre-season and my coaching staff was aware of the affect this death had on me, I was allowed to take an extra day to be with my family.

The ride home with my mother was very quiet as I stared into space, reminiscing on the memories I shared with my friend. His parents were a part of my mother, aunt, and uncle's tribe, so it only made sense that when my friend and I were produced, we would share the same kinship. We went to the same nursery, elementary, middle, and high school. Our parents' homes were right down the street from one another, so he walked to my house each morning so my mother could take us to the bus stop. We were conjoined at the hip. Every weekend, we would ride our bikes, play video games, and play basketball together after I watched 'Soul Train' with my neighbors. Our favorite memory was my mother taking us to the 'Midnight Basketball League' games downtown when we were in middle school. We watched intensely, picking on any player that could not play the game and remembering the impressive moves of the top players to imitate later on my basketball goal.

Towards the end of middle school, into high school, our environment started to change, and we were old enough to recognize it. Shiloh became a place where it was easy to embark on the wrong path if you were not particular of the company you kept and where you hung out. I continued to stay focused on basketball, and I saw my friend a little less outside of school. A distance was created between us with a clear understanding of why, but we always remained tribe. My first few years at Limestone, we spoke sporadically as he tried to figure out what he wanted to do in life. I currently harbored a sense of guilt that I did not make myself available enough to support him during this time. We briefly reconnected in the summer before his tragic death, when we discovered we worked at the same summer camp. The satisfying part was how we picked up where we left off, never missing a beat with fun times and gut-wrenching laughs. He remained, and always will be, my best friend, my tribe, and my brother, a bond forever anchoring a place in my heart for as long as I live.

When I returned to Limestone, I was medically cleared to resume basketball activities. It took a few days for me to regain my wind and get my legs back under me. One day before practice, my head coach told me that I needed to come and see him before I took the floor. When I got there, I approached him with caution, as I assumed this was pertaining to my grades... again. Instead, he informed me that I had been selected for the Division II Pre-Season All-American team, the first in Limestone Women's Basketball history. Despite my internal turmoil, I was elated. I had accomplished a lot in two years, but I never imagined that anyone would be able to place "All-American" beside my name. This title confirmed and solidified my place in the history books.

When people ask me, "Which year was your favorite year at Limestone, in regards to the basketball team?" My answer is, and will always remain, the 2011-2012 team. Our depth and experience set us apart from every team in the conference, and we were now viewed as the top tier. We were accomplished upperclassmen who'd been through the trials and triumphs of each season, growing into our greatness each step of the way. Each of our returning players took the summer to improve upon their games, and with the addition of a few talented freshman and a junior college transfer, we acquired a perfect balance. With the overall improvement of our team, some of the offensive load was taken off my shoulders. I stumbled out of the gates in my first two games, with a few low scoring outputs. I failed to find a rhythm early, after missing a month of pre-season preparation. Things began to click in the fourth game of the season, and I averaged nineteen points per game going into Christmas break.

My relationship with my team was as good as could be expected. The individuals I had a few conflicts with in the previous years left words unspoken. We never clashed again, but we hardly spoke about things that were not directly related to basketball. I was able to bond with our new teammates as I tried to be open to developing new friendships with fresh starts. During Christmas break, I reaggravated my foot injury, which sidelined me for two weeks, causing me to miss a game. This gave me ample time to think about some things in my life. Prior to my injury, I had an in-depth conversation with one of my teammates regarding our team. What resonated with me was her point of view on our coaches' "favoritism" and how this affected some of the other team members. Until this conversation, I never paid much attention to it. My teammate illustrated one scenario that my team had a problem with.

She reminded me that I'd missed championship week, but was still allowed to start and play in our games. Championship week was the very last week of pre-season, where you were required to pass our conditioning tests to play in live action games. If you did not pass a test, you had to run the test over until you made your time. With the timing of my injury coinciding with the death of my best friend, I failed to run during this week. It was my initial understanding that I would be required to run on our off days, since official practice had begun, but ultimately, this was decided against because I needed my off days to recover. I soaked in my teammate's statement, and there was nothing I could say. I was not going to do anything I was not made to do. The decision was made that I did not have to complete championship week, and I was not punished as often for missing class. I accepted the fact that my teammates harbored some resentment towards me for essentially being able to do what I wanted, when I wanted, with little to no consequences.

Again, this was where leadership, rather my lack thereof, was visible again. A true leader would have taken it upon herself to make sure she made up what was missed to prevent this type of indignation within the team. I was not a leader, and I was not in a place with some my team where they cared to express their feelings to me. They tried that once, and I left them with nothing. I openly received her words, but there was nothing I could do, scratch that, nothing I was willing to do to change that. I certainly was not about to do championship week this deep in the season, and I was not confident enough to admit my faults.

Having useless time was the only opportunity I took to really reflect on where I was in my life. Often, I knew I was not doing the right things, but I was not stable enough to change anything, and I always knew I had basketball. I failed my General Biology course because of non-attendance, missed quizzes, and tests. It was expected, as I could count on one hand how many times I'd reported to that class after my friend's passing. For the very first time in my academic career, my back was against the wall. I was placed on academic probation with the risk of suspension and ineligibility for my senior season. My reality was simple: maintain a 3.0 for the spring semester or lose everything.

When I returned to the court, I was replaced in the starting line-up by one of our talented freshman. At first, it didn't bother me because I had missed a few weeks of practice and a game; so, I agreed with coaches' decision. It began to aggravate me when three became four, four became five, five became six, six became seven games, and I was still coming off the bench. Not only was I a pre-season All-American coming off the bench, I was still leading our team in scoring coming off the bench in reduced minutes. I felt disrespected by my coach because it was absurd for me to come off the bench with my productivity. I could understand one or two games, but twelve games was unacceptable. Yes, we won eleven of those twelve games, but I was not happy about my reduced role.

Yes, my teammate could shine in her moment, but I was not going to take a back seat to someone who could not match or surpass my productivity. Part of me tried to be okay with the circumstance, because of my special treatment from the coaching staff, but the other part felt like he was going too far to prove a point. I expressed my frustration towards my coach with my mother, who outwardly expressed her sentiments to the coaching staff. I did not fully agree with her actions, but she expressed the feelings I could not say to him myself. I was reinserted into the starting lineup after we lost the twelfth game of our streak and after we struggled at the start of a few games. My visible frustration and my mother expressing her discontent drove a wedge between my coach and I that remained for the foreseeable future.

Once I was back in the starting lineup, we finished the regular season strongly, winning the Conference Carolinas regular season championship, the first in Limestone Women's basketball history. We also received the #1 seed heading into the conference tournament. There was no doubt in our minds that we were the best team in the conference, and we all understood it was our time. We were ready to take what was rightfully ours.

I felt great going into the tournament. I was named First Team All-Conference again. Physically, I felt fresh, and I was prepared to have an all-time great performance. We made light work of our first-round opponent, who fought hard but were simply outmatched. Our second-round opponent was a familiar foe—Mt. Olive. They gave us their usual fight, but my twenty-five points, in addition to my teammates having equally great performances, was no match by the end of the game. In the Conference championship, we met our biggest rival, Barton College. Barton owned our conference in my earlier years, but it was now our turn to dethrone them from the top. Both teams held a mutual respect, but we strongly disliked each other.

Each time we played Barton, it was a basketball version of a street fight. There was a lot of trash talk, extra pushes after the play was dead, and a few skirmishes throughout the game. Barton tried, but never prevailed in intimidating us. Yes, we respect you, but you are not going to run over us, nor get into one our faces without us having that person's back. They gave us extra motivation coming into the championship game, as we discovered they were using their social media services to trash talk on how they were going to win this championship on our home floor...okay.

We already knew what to expect, and we prepared ourselves accordingly. Barton was one of the very few teams we ever played zone against. Their athleticism was off the charts, but their inability to make outside jump shots fell right into our hands. All we had to do was force contested jumpers, control the defensive boards, and keep them off the free throw line. Playing our brand of basketball had gotten us this far, and we were not going to change that now. We forced Barton to play Limestone basketball, and there was no way to compete with that. They made us fight and scrap for every positive play we made in that game, but it made our victory that much sweeter. Yet again, my team and I made history and solidified our place in the record books, a feat that would bind us together, forever. We were now a part of something bigger than ourselves.

In the 2011-2012 season, we brought the first regular season conference championship to Limestone and capped it off by winning the conference tournament championship, automatically earning us the first NCAA tournament berth in Limestone Women's basketball history. I was named the conference tournament Most Valuable Player, another first in program history, and another form of validation within my sport. We went on to lose to Lander University in the first round of the NCAA tournament. The way Lander was structured, was equivalent to us looking in the mirror. This game was one of the very few times we lost to a better team. When the last buzzer rang, I dropped my head in disappointment as we went through the line to shake our opponents' hands. When I was face-to-face with Lander's coach, he offered words of reassurance. It felt great to know that people outside of Limestone and my hometown took notice of my accomplishments, even during defeat. I found my mother in the stands after the game, and she held me tight in a lengthy embrace. She reiterated how proud she was of me, but her exiting words put everything back in focus. "You had a great year, but it is now over. Now, you need to defeat your last battle." My academics.

The spring semester of my junior year was the best semester I'd had academically up until that point. Knowing that basketball was hanging in the balance, I understood my dire circumstances. I didn't skip my classes. I was alert and present during lessons, and I sought help when I felt I needed it. My junior year ended, and my spring semester grade point average was a 3.1, easily lifting probation off my name. My senior year was no longer in jeopardy. I was proud of myself for executing the necessary effort required to achieve classroom success. When word traveled throughout campus, within the coaches, and faculty members, some were genuinely happy for me because they believed in my potential. Others were very passive aggressive in their praise. These individuals displayed their thoughts about me from the stereotypical black athlete. Some people really believed that I lacked the necessary intelligence to excel academically. I had the nerve to ask myself why they had these thoughts about me. Then, I remembered it was because I internalized everything people thought I was, not everything I quietly aspired to be.

During an exit meeting with my advisor, he explained that, although I had a superb spring semester, I was not on schedule to graduate the following May because of previously failed courses and major requirements I had yet to fulfill. I talked to my mother about my advisor's meeting, and she suggested that I enroll in summer school to retake the failed courses and get a head start on some requirements I kept putting to the side. We moved ahead with these plans, and as I was in an orientation appointment, I informed my head coach of my plan to start summer school. He advised against it. He explained that all my courses would not transfer over, and that, if I did poorly in the summer classes, it would affect my overall GPA and could possibly put me at risk for ineligibility again.

There are a couple things to acknowledge right here. First, I should have trusted my instinct to move forward with summer school. I should have taken the initiative to retain all the proper information needed to ensure my courses would indeed transfer to Limestone. Secondly, I should have taken my coach's lack of confidence in me as motivation in these summer classes, and show him that no matter what he thought, I would make sure I passed these courses in the face of his "worry." This was a chance for me to make a decision for myself that had nothing to do with basketball, but everything to do with my future, and I did not. I rested in the box of complacency. I was already eligible for the next season, so like my coach suggested, why take the risk? This was a glaring example of me accepting someone else's low expectation for my life. My coach had no faith in me in the moment because of my track record, and it deflated my own confidence in what I wanted to do this summer hearing apprehension from him. I accepted it and after my stellar semester, I began to doubt if I could repeat it. The people around me doubted this as well. For years, I showed them that I had one focus, and eventually they believed it was all I was. Just when I felt a light shift in my mindset, I fell deeper into my blindness. Not attending summer school deflated my mother, as she grew tired of the same vicious cycle and her frustration was starting to reveal itself.

9

Uncertain

My life became one living and breathing dysfunction. After numerous years of questionable decisions, and a subpar academic standing, my foundation had cracked. I began to feel like in outsider in the place I'd called home for the past three years. My teammates had shown tremendous internal growth and evolvement, their conversations were rooted in their plans after graduation, and how they were relieved that their senior year would be relatively easy. Some of the conflict that separated some team members had been worked through, and with five incoming freshmen, my fellow seniors slid seamlessly into the roles of mentors, grooming the next stars to pick up the torch and continue pushing the program forward. These feelings and conversations, I simply could not be a part of. I insolated deeper into consistent friendships and spent increasing time away from my team. A lot of my teammates developed friendships with regular students, our student government council, and members of various teams. They embraced a variety of different experiences outside of basketball, and I remained known only for my talent. I was cordial with everyone, never rude but hardly open, not close enough to expose any part of myself that was not related to basketball.

I realized I now had a difficult time relating to my teammates because they'd evolved into spaces I had yet to access. I was a stranger in a place of familiarity. My inner circle became inapplicable because of their personal strides and victories. My lack of development over the years left me behind, and I did not know where to search for answers. I wanted to do and be better, but I lacked the understanding of how to achieve that goal. Again, I turned to the one object that had remained consistent this entire time. I put so much into this object, that the only time I could say I was truly happy was when I held it in my hands: basketball.

This pre-season was one of hard work and preparation going into my final season. I was crowned an Division II All-American honorable mention and the usual hype surrounded my team and I as the season began. This second All-American status was placed beside my name before knowing that this season would be the worst statistical output of my career. During the pre-season scrimmages and first live game action, I picked up where I left off in my junior season, outstanding shooting performances in combination with my team propelling us to numerous lopsided victories. Soon after the start of the season, my production hit a brick wall. My jump shot no longer fell, my mid-range game fluctuated, and I had all but erased my ability to put the ball on the floor. My confidence was fleeting and my body felt like I couldn't do the things that made me an all-time great. I totaled two twenty-point games in our first seventeen games, a far cry from the prolific scorer I was known to be.

Consider this, my fellow seniors approached this season as a do-or-die circumstance, and they were playing the best basketball of their careers. Different from previous years, I did not have to lead them in scoring every night for us to be successful. There were countless times during my senior season that I was a role player with the starting spot. Understand how this impacted me. When basketball was the one thing that I truly identified with, sharing recognition in a space that I was accustomed to exclusively occupying caused me to fold deeper into myself and own a feeling of not being needed. I was happy for my teammates being able to blossom and thrive, they earned and deserved that opportunity. But without hearing my normal validation, I felt I had nothing. It was not that I did not want to share the spotlight; I just did not know how, without drowning in my rain.

My relationship with my mother was strained during this period, which only furthered my implosion. Years of worrying about my academics, falling short of her hopes for me, throwing away my intelligence, making decisions that altered my future, and essentially throwing away a golden opportunity she sacrificed so much to create, took a mental and emotional toll on her. She was no longer proud of the athletic accomplishments. She was utterly disappointed in me and the direction my life was headed. Our conversations were not as frequent, daily conversations dwindled down to once, maybe twice a week. When we did speak, often we began to argue about me not taking control over my life, but me actually believing I had.

She eventually stopped traveling to my games because of our discord. You must understand that, up until I went to college, my mother NEVER missed one of my games. In my earlier seasons, I had to tell her that she did not have to travel to a school that was a two-hour drive from Asheville during the week to see me play. That was the lengths she went to show her love and support of me. Now, I looked in those stands and didn't see her, feel her presence, or see her smile; it crushed me. She was my backbone and my crutch. If I was having a bad game, I could glance up to her for extra motivation, and she would give a wink or a nod telling me that I was okay. That disappeared, and though I tried to convince myself every day that I would be fine, I knew it was a lie. Unfairly, I briefly reconnected with my father during this time, trying to fill the void of missing my mother. I love my father, but he could not fill that hole in my heart if he lived three lifetimes. I am thankful for everything he did and tried to do for me in this time, but no true healing happened, because the foundation of which I contacted him was not authentic. I just wanted a parent's love.

I was disappearing internally, fading into a shell of a person. I had moments where I was smiling and laughing with some teammates. Then, moments later, I cried for no apparent reason. But, it was because I was fractured. I tried to use the game to fuse my brokenness, but that didn't work for me anymore, possibly because the game was not the same as it once was. Statistically, my team was having the best season in program history, but I was not as thrilled as I should've been. My demoralization was now spilling over into the one area that was supposed to be sacred. Instead of allowing myself to completely drown, I found myself having to regroup before each practice and game, to mask my personal turmoil from the outside world. I tried to salvage my senior season and leave the game the same way I lived it in my previous seasons, in prominence.

In our final twelve games, I scored over twenty points in seven of them. Despite how I felt, my talent remained superior to the opponents I faced. I will admit, in my senior season, I did not work as hard as I once did because my mental and emotional state presented a real disinterest in life, but I showed flashes of my former self in this last stretch of games. I found it was not as pleasing as it once was. Statistically I recovered some ground from my lack of production early on, but I will always feel that my team carried me through that season more than they can understand. I extended what I could give from game to game, but because they stepped up and grew in confidence, we were propelled to new heights as a basketball program.

We secured a consecutive Conference Carolinas regular season championship, but fell in the semi-finals of the conference tournament to familiar foe Mt. Olive. Because of our two-loss record and our strong non-conference schedule, we were granted an at-large bid to the NCAA tournament—another historic landmark to be placed by our names. I was named Second Team All-Conference Carolinas and two of my teammates were named to the First Team for the first time in their careers; a well-deserved honor for the type of year those ladies accumulated. I made history again as the only women's player to be named to an all-conference team all four years. And, history was not done with me...

We worked hard to prepare for the NCAA tournament as we faced Barton in the first round. A strong balanced attack on both ends of the floor launched us into the second round to face another conference opponent in Pfeiffer. Entering this match-up, I was thirteen points away from breaking the programs all-time leading scorer record. Throughout my career, I had a history of having monster games versus this opponent. While talented, guarding my athleticism was problematic, and this game would not be any different. I scored nineteen first half points, breaking the scoring record in the first ten minutes of the game. I finished the game with twenty-five points. With the normal contributions from my teammates, we easily advance to the Sweet Sixteen. This is the furthest a team had advanced in this moment. Breaking the scoring record was the highlight of my career. All my blood, sweat, and tears were worth that feeling. I placed my internal struggles to the side and allowed myself to present in my moment. When I started this journey, I was prepared to be a role player, never undervalued, but not a superstar. My wildest dream did not look like this and my expectations were never this high. I expected to be successful, but I did not know this was the type of success God planned for me.

The school, fans, coaches, and most importantly, my teammates congratulated me one-by-one. In the post-game interview, I made it a point to speak about my teammates and how none of this would have been possible without them. I said those words knowing in my heart it was what I truly believed. Despite the drama and the lows, our good times and positive experiences always outweighed the negativity. There would be no Maria "Shiloh" Young without every teammate I played beside from 2009 to 2013.

The round of thirty-two match-up was my last shining moment in a Limestone College uniform. We play #1 seeded Clayton State in the Sweet Sixteen. Although my teammates had very memorable games, the inconsistency I displayed most of the season resurfaced in this game. Clayton State was a powerhouse, and we needed everyone's best performance to overcome them, but in the end, we fell short. Tears streamed down my face as my head coach approached each senior, embraced them, and shared a word of encouragement. As he embraced me, I allowed my tears to flow freely.

"You have had a special career," he said. Although our relationship was tested, I felt our embrace was more than coach to player, but one of family. As we exited the locker room, our team was showered with an abundance of love from all of our supporters, a love I desperately needed, fear-ing I would never feel it again. As a team, we congratulated each other on all of our accomplishments, as I was not the only individual from my team who would live in the record books. I shared moments of kinship with them that I hadn't felt in quite some time. A gleam of optimism shone through that all these relationships would travel back to the foundation that brought us together in the beginning. I proceeded to one of the seats in the very back of the bus and slid into the seat right next to the window.

Maria "Shiloh" Young

2013 • Limestone Women's Basketball All-Time Leading Scorer

2013 • Most Career Three Pointers Made in Limestone Women's Basketball (307)

2013 • Second Team All-Conference Carolinas

2012-13 • Women's Division II Bulletin Super Sixteen Pre-season All-American Honorable Mention

2012 • Conference Carolinas Tournament Most Valuable Player

2012 • Conference Carolinas All-Tournament Team

2011-12 • First-Team All-Conference Carolinas

2011-12 • Conference Carolinas Player of the Week

2011-12 • Women's Division II Bulletin Super Sixteen Pre-season All-American

2011-12 • Nationally ranked in points per game (50th – 16.9), three-pointers per game (3rd – 3.61) and three-point percentage (10th – 42.4%)

2011 • Conference Carolinas All-Tournament Team
2010-11 • First-Team All-Conference Carolinas
2010-11 • Conference Carolinas Scoring Champion
2010-11 • Conference Carolinas Player of the Week
2010-11 • Nationally ranked in points per game (10th – 19.5), three-points per game (10th – 3.0), and three-point percentage (15th – 42.8%)
2009-10 • Conference Carolinas Freshman of the Year
2009-10 • Second-Team All-Conference Carolinas

I also reflect on the young women I created history with and what we accomplished. We laid the foundation and offered a blueprint of greatness for the next class; something for the ones who followed to abide by. We brought multiple championships and NCAA tournament appearances to a program that was barely a .500 team prior to our arrival. We turned a middle of the pack program into a powerhouse few teams could match. Our love for the game, program, and each other allowed us to leave our differences at the door and come together when we needed each other the most. Every last one of us brought our own unique greatness to the program, which was why I was not the only player from this class in the grasp of history. We were bound to each other through our historic rise. We set a precedent that remains engraved in the fabric of Limestone Women's basketball to this day, and the young women who came after us have now made their own history. Our time as Limestone players closed, but we sparked a new era of domination.

I began to cry silently, tears of joy and pain. My glorious career was officially over. I was overjoyed about the accom-

plishments, but now thrust into facing my emotional instabili-
ty. I had no clue about what my future held, and I was terrified
about where I would end up. What would become of me? I
called the one person I desired to lean on, my mother.

10

Foreign Feelings

Relationships have, and continue to be, an area of my life left unmastered. I have exceptional love and relationship examples in my family, with my aunts and uncles having been married for thirty plus years. Although I have this wonderful model, I seldom use it in my personal life. My family has taught me in abundance, but I remain green on aspects related to developing and maintaining a relationship. After years of the annoying questions, "Why don't you bring someone home?" and "Are we ever going to see you with anyone?" I suppressed my thoughts, fears, and questions about love and relationships. I simply desired to just be.

In my twenty-six years, I have had two real relationships, both of which began and concluded during my time at Limestone. While having immense success as an athlete, I found myself alone and yearning for a deeper connection. It is very cliché, but as a star player, I wanted someone to share my success with. I told myself that I was ready for love and relationships. I repeated it enough until I actually believed I was. If you asked me what I brought to a relationship that directly related to its longevity, I could not tell you. You cannot bring something to the table that you are not aware you have.

The fantasy of love and a relationship was beautiful, but the reality was nothing short of a disaster. I could not make my first relationship a priority, and I honestly did not want to. Between practice, games, school, and traveling dominating my schedule, I did not want to exclude any of my fun or include my relationship in it. I would disregard plans, to attend campus parties, ignore calls and texts, and go weeks without visiting or having an authentic conversation. Before you read these next sentences, I am informing you that I extend a free pass to judge me.

You may be wondering how or why I did not show remorse for my actions. The reason is, I would refer to one of my favorite songs by one of my favorite R&B groups, New Edition, entitled "Leaving you again." The chorus is as follows:

I'm leaving you again

And I thought I'd tell you when

I know how you must feel

But if your loves for real

You'll try to understand

That I'm back in popular demand

I allow you to let the judging commence. I did not allow myself to make this relationship a priority because I was not willing to change my lifestyle to include anyone else, and no feelings outside of my own mattered. The foolish part was, despite my actions, I expected my relationship to never change as I claimed it was "love." Years removed from this relationship, I realize that at twenty years old, atop of my pedestal at its highest peak and barely knowing myself, I was unprepared for what a relationship required, while protecting the little I did know about myself—protecting all I wanted and hoped to be. I ducked face-to-face encounters, shackled by the fear of awkwardness. I withheld significant conversations, shackled by the fear of acceptance, and suppressed honest feelings, shackled by the fear of them falling unshared. All of these were defense mechanisms I used without having a valid reason to do so. I protected my best self because I did not know how to live in it for the both of us.

IN DEFENSE OF ME

Mind in defense mode

Conditioned to protect myself from the unknown

I know how this story goes

Everything is good until imperfections become apparent

The reason why some "bonds" came and went

The weakest part of me

All I hope to be, sworn in secrecy

True and false insecurities

Questioning sincerity

Intrigued by me?

"No, you couldn't be"

See that's the defense in me

Protecting the best part of me

"Hasn't been enough time"

See that's the defense in me

Protecting the best part of me

"Is there an underline?"

See that's the defense in me

Protecting the best part of me

But on the flip side

Maybe you truly empathize

And understand the things I see from my eyes

Maybe I'm all you say I am to you

And the more I get out of my own way I'll see that fact as true

Navigating new terrain failing to explain what's happening in my brain

Sunshine is easy, but what happens when it rains

Can I maintain?

Can this sustain?

85

These questions echo heavily when I feel the weakest parts of me so vividly

Vulnerability is hard for me and I cannot build without being free

Do I know what the future holds?

No

The only thing I'm sure of is the exceptional person I know

Lord, it's me

I did not take this seriously

Nor cherished all it could be.

I missed out on what we hoped to be

One day, I hope I can forgive me.

The second and final relationship was completely different as I went from one extreme to the other. I did not make the first one a priority, and I made this relationship too much of one. I attempted to learn from my past mistakes without completely turning over a new leaf. Makes sense, right? I did not think so. Although I tried, I never completely altered my ways of old, but I sought validation for my effort, that I did not always receive. As an insecure person in relationships, I needed a lot of assurance that I was doing something, anything right, and it became taxing. The lack of complete change, in addition to inadequate feelings on both streets, created a volatile and fractured infrastructure that was doomed from the beginning. I did not completely close door number one before walking into door number two. I over compensated in the offering of attention, in an effort to right wrongs, and again, because I believed I was in love.

I isolated myself from my friends with the belief that my relationship had to be at the top of my list, and I sacrificed a piece of my happiness. I did not have sufficient balance and this bred an unhealthy connection to this individual. The more time I put into this relationship, the more alone I became. Not because my friends lost care or betrayed me. It was because I disappeared on them. I told myself this was the price of being in love, but it was not supposed to be this hard. My love was not real love at all. It was my idea of what I perceived love to be. No, this relationship was not all bad, but the good moments were few and far between. The dissolving of this happened long before the actual nail was put in our coffin, but we tried to hold onto it out of love, not realizing it was already gone. I was devastated for some time after we went our separate ways, because I was alone and detached from the things and people I enjoyed.

"LOVE"

Our "bond" was never healthy

The toxicity almost proved to be deadly

I don't know the moment I fell or how

My mind couldn't stop what my heart would allow

Our foundation was weak

The future was bleak

We weren't standing on faith and friendship

Only mistrust and arguments that were senseless

I wasn't trustworthy or ready for love

*Relationships require sacrifice and parts of me I couldn't give
up*

Our relationship was confusing

We were losing, but letting you go

I'm refusing

Trying to salvage a love that was gone from the start

I lost myself and desires of my heart

Thank you for giving up on me

Thank you for giving up on us

Thank you forcing me to see what I ignored all along

Our love was wrong.

In hindsight, in reflection, I was connected to a false idea of what love was. Love is supposed to—and when I say supposed to, this is what I would like for love to do for me—present a feeling of freedom. Two friends committed to building a foundation that will sustain them through great challenges. Where honesty, loyalty, and respect are intertwined in the fabric. Where the glue is both the individuals' faith in the Most High, and His grace, mercy, and peace. Love does not make you feel trapped in a box you do not have the strength to climb out of. It does not make you feel inadequate, unworthy, or envious. It never compromises the brightest parts of your soul to ensure that you do not outshine the person next to you. Love is pure, love is kind, love is the God in you.

At twenty-six, I remain removed from love and relationships. As I have grown, I have come to understand that my relationship failures stem from not holding myself accountable for not knowing. I never sought answers to my questions, and I never took the time to develop Maria first. Love starts inside a happy being. At twenty-six I am aware of the qualities I own, and what I can bring to a relationship, but I do not see this in the near future for three reasons:

Number one—will and ambition:
The will and ambition to want and be more. These two words have held me prisoner for the moment. Discovering new passions has inspired me to wear many hats. I find it difficult to balance my job and personal aspirations. It is hard for me to include someone in this when I have set my goals high, and through faith and hard work, I intend to achieve each one of them. Most importantly, I enjoy doing so.

Number two—lack of commitment:

I choose not to commit myself to something I have little to no desire in developing. Relationships can be wonderful, but they require a mutual effort, and that is something I cannot put forth. Being aware of this fact prevents me from treating someone unfairly. I want to be able to give all of me when I take that step, and at this point, I am not ready.

Number three—fear:

A feeling I have yet to master and barely tolerate. My biggest fear is offering all I have to give and it still not be enough. I am fearful of taking years of life lessons and growth, applying it, and still falling short of what the relationship could be.

As I have illustrated, this area of my life signifies unsteady waters I continue to navigate each day. Although I do not have all the subsequent answers to my questions, and this aspect of my life remains my biggest uncertainty, this is what I do know: I have only truly known myself for four years, and the depth of my complexities are shattered stained glass being fused together to display a sublime portrait. The further I travel in my journey, and the more I continue to stay committed to my personal development, the more that clarity finds me at the point I am seeking it, in God's time.

11

Troubled Waters

Over the past four years, I've developed the unhealthy traits of suppression and isolation. I suppressed my thoughts, feelings, concerns, and isolated myself because I did not want to be vulnerable or be viewed as "weak" for showing emotion. I believed that I could handle my conflictions on my own because I was taught to be strong—not realizing my anguish only advanced my seclusion.

In the spring semester of my senior year, I completely stopped going to class. When I say completely stopped, I mean, stopped showing up to the classroom and no homework, quizzes, or tests were turned in. The only obligations met during this time were the ones that dealt with basketball, as I silently suffered on my own. When my career at Limestone was over, I dove further into societal separation, terrified of what would happen next. I was not prepared for life after basketball, and the thought of not playing this game never entered my mind. For the last seventeen years, this game had been my life. I knew I was not going to graduate with my class nor my teammates, and the feelings of guilt and shame washed over me because I knew it was no one's fault but my own. I was in this situation because I never prepared a plan B.

Questioning how to move forward, one more opportunity to play basketball was extended to me, and I jumped at it because I had no alternative. While navigating my mental and emotional distress, I got a small boost of energy when a friend of mine who played at Queens University put me in contact with his agent, whom negotiated a deal for him to play professional basketball in Germany. I made contact with some family and friends that played, or were currently playing, overseas for their input, advice, and possible contacts. Normally, your collegiate coaching staff would assist in this process, but my coaching staff and I had not seen or spoken to each other much after the conclusion of my senior season—by my choice. Pride would not allow me to ask for their help. After networking for a few weeks, and consulting with some of my family, I signed a deal with an agent and accepted an invitation to an exposure camp in New Hampshire—scheduled for later that summer.

This should have been a joyous occasion for me, since I signed a deal and was one step closer to playing professional basketball, but it wasn't, for two main reasons. One, the young women I arrived on campus with, along with my childhood tribe, were preparing for graduation and tackling the real world, off to begin a new chapter in their lives, ready to receive all the blessings God had waiting for them on the other side of commencement. They were shining examples of what student athletes were supposed to be. As with our senior and school wide awards banquet, I opted to skip the graduation ceremony, sparing myself the embarrassment of wondering eyes. Two, part of me only signed this deal because I saw no alternative. I did not graduate and there was no Limestone Women's Basketball for me to come back to. The feelings of pain, anger, shame, worthlessness, and defeat become too much for me to suppress anymore.

As I was arriving back on campus one day, I abruptly pulled my car over into a parking lot. I pulled my phone out and called my mother. As soon as she answered the phone, I became hysterical and verbalized everything that had been eating away at my sanity. I was finally honest with her about my academic standing. Being that our relationship had become rocky over the past five to six months, I fully expected her to yell and scream, "I told you so!" or "What you crying for now?!" But, she didn't. She said, "Maria, where you find yourself right now is a mirror of how things have always been. You like to learn lessons the hard way, but you are finding out that your life is no longer a game. Take your exams, come home, and we will figure this out together." That was exactly what I did.

I returned to Asheville in the spring of 2013, defeated and ashamed, but to the outside world, everything looked fine. A lot of people thought I was home to prepare for going overseas—which was partially true—but they did not know I was a year off from graduating. My tribe was under the impression that I would be crossing the stage in December of 2013. As unlikely as it was, I opted to tell them at a later time. Several of my family members hold Bachelors, Masters, and Doctorate degrees from some of the most prestigious institutions of higher learning in the country. Though they never verbalized their disappointment to me, I knew they felt it, and I did not want to add these feelings on top of what I was already struggling with. I told my mother I wanted to try the overseas showcase because it could produce a great opportunity for me. I made sure she knew that if I was signed by a team, I would still pursue my degree through Limestone's online program. Reluctantly, she agreed. My mother was never a fan of me going to a different country, and she most certainly was not happy about my academic standing, but she agreed I would not know how things would turn out unless I went to this showcase.

A month later, my mom and I flew to New Hampshire. There were over 150 players from all around the country. I was able to see some familiar faces. I recognized several players I'd played against in college. The showcase was over two days, and I played well. I did not put myself through vigorous workouts prior to this camp, but I was still able to illustrate my offensive repertoire and my willingness to play defense. I showcased everything that made me one the best players to ever come through Limestone College's Women's Basketball program.

Upon the conclusion of the camp, my agent was contacted by teams in Germany and Portugal. I contained my excitement, as I had noticed constant, severe pain in my left knee since returning from the showcase. I tried several days of heat and ice treatments, but nothing could subdue that pain. After a few weeks of no improvement, I went to the doctor who examined me and advised that I needed an MRI. I had to inform my agent of this news, and soon after, the basketball teams in Germany and Portugal ceased their talks with him. My MRI results came back and it was determined that I had torn my patella tendon, and it requires surgery with a six to eight month recovery period.

My world was obliterated, and now I had to come to terms with the reality that my basketball career had officially come to an end. I had surgery in the coming days and came completely unraveled. Still reeling from the death of an uncle who held my fondest memories, it is unbeknownst to my family that I am on academic probation again. Since it was my third time on probation, it was categorized as academic suspension. Meaning, there was a strong possibility that I would be suspended from Limestone for the fall semester of 2013 and not able to resume any studies until 2014 on special provisions. If I could explain my poor spring semester, my fate would be left in the hands of an administration board that could approve my return in the fall, if my explanation is satisfactory. I held this secret to my heart, until the day I wrote this section of this book. I could not bare to see the disappointment on the faces of my family if they knew the position I was in. That disapproval would have pierced my soul in a way I couldn't tolerate.

In the days after surgery, I found myself in the deepest depths of despair. I didn't eat, I couldn't sleep, and there were days when I didn't leave my bed or my room. I lay in the dark, crying silent tears, and wishing I could simply disappear. There were several nights that I held my bottle of pain medication, contemplating whether I wanted live. I asked myself, *what is your purpose here in this life?* The only thing I felt I had ever been great at was snatched from me, so why should I remain here to face that shame? You have no purpose, and that means you have no life. I descended to the bottom of my mental, emotional, and spiritual rung, trying to slowly will myself to leave this life behind. I did not feel worthy enough, and I was struggling to find a reason to live. The embarrassment of "another black athlete" fallen from grace, and my current academic suspension, enhanced my pessimism. I slid into depths I did not feel I could come back from. My faith was broken, and I did not have a foundation to stand on. I was tired—tired of feeling these emotions, and I wanted to make the noise stop. Lying in that bed, with a machine bending my knee for me eight to nine hours a day, forced me to experience everything I ever suppressed, and it pushed me to the brink of contemplating ending my life.

One night, in the midst of this storm, my mother walked into my room. I tried to wipe my tears away to hide how upset I was, but as always, a mother knows. She walked over to my bed and extended her hand to me. I grabbed her and one of my crutches to help me stand. When I made it to my feet, my mother pulled me into her embrace. No words were spoken for a few moments, as she allowed me to release. My hands were uneasy, my body shaking, and all my weight was supported by my mother's body. As my sobs began to slow, my mother said, "God is still here, and you are not done!" She embraced me again and helped me back into my bed. As she exited the room, she gave me a half-moon smile and a nod. Did my mother hold underlying anger and disappointment in me? Yes. Did my mother forget the position I was in? No. Did my mother cry at night sometimes thinking about how I devalued my education? Yes, but what makes my mother so special is that she knew I did not need to hear any negativity or belittling from her. She did not offer me a sharp tongue. She gave me her unconditional love. She reminded me that she was ready to help me pick up the pieces of my life, and most importantly, she reminded me that God was still in control. I went into prayer, a practice I mistakenly stepped away from over the past year.

"Dear Lord, it's me. I come to you in this hour broken, confused, and fearful of what to do. I feel no purpose and lack direction. I am in a valley that I see no way out of. I have blood on my hands—the blood of pride, conceit, entitlement, arrogance, and disregard. I am tired, I am weak, but I seek your love and guidance. I surrender my all to you, in faith that I may be restored. Assist me in discovering parts of myself left unrevealed and regaining direction in where my life is supposed to go. Help me to

see your purpose for me because in you lies my victory, healing, and breakthrough. Reveal my true self to me in your way and by your will, amen.

I felt like a spiritual burden had been lifted from my shoulders. I was still in the forest, but I now had the faith and hope that there would be light to reveal itself on the other side. My foundation of faith, family, and fellowship was beginning to rebuild. In the next few days, I finally took the time to respond to friends and teammates who extended prayers and well wishes to me after my surgery. The significance of this moment cannot be overstated. After the college season concluded, and my professional debut never came to fruition, I thought people would forget about me. I thought that I would have faded into the background because I no longer possessed basketball prominence, and I withdrew for most of my senior year. This showed me that there was life after basketball and that there were people who cared about the shape my life would take.

My older brother, who at this time was a resident of Washington D.C, sent me a text message that sparked the new direction my life was about to take. It was the beginning of reconstructing our closeness to one another. The text message read: *"I know you're a little discouraged about not being able to play ball again, but know God always has a plan, and it may be something you least expect. You left your mark, you left the game on top. Now, it's time to take on this game called life."* My brother was right. I did leave my mark, and I did leave the game on top. Nothing was ever going to change that fact, but it was time to move on and let go of the "hoop dream." Not because I was not capable, but because God was telling me it was time. My brother, in this moment, represented what my tribe always conveyed—the ability to help me pick up the pieces and help me regain stability when I stumbled.

It was one event that touched me the most during this dark period, and that was when my tribe threw me a "Cheer-Up Cookout." It was unannounced and very much unexpected, but they showed up at my grandmother's home, as loud as ever, ready to have a great time. They were not aware of the intensity of the pain I was feeling, but they knew of my discouragement and how it was taking a toll on me. I will never know what they felt internally during these days, but they illustrated that no matter the obstacles my life presented, they still loved and supported me. They pulled the grill on two wheels under the carport, sat chairs around a blue card table, set up small speakers playing my favorite 70's tunes, and helped me outside to enjoy the fellowship with them. We laughed, we sang, and they danced. We engage in friendly arguments over spade games, and reminisced about the "Old Shiloh and Swannanoa" days. For a few hours, nothing else mattered—only my family and I enjoying a simple evening of fellowship.

Before leaving, my aunt gifted me with a book she encouraged me to read entitled, "The Miseducation of the Negro" written by black history month founder, Dr. Carter G. Woodson. She told me that there were some valuable lessons and information within this book that I would find very interesting and helpful. Before this time, I had not read much literature outside of what was required in my classes, but the area of African American history was always able to capture and keep my attention. These were the classes over my high school and college academic career that I displayed the most success in. The moment I began to read this book, the ideals never rendered their hold on me.

Miseducation introduced me to ideas that forced me to raise questions about myself, reflect on the decisions I made, and inspired me to study in-depth about my education and the system I inherited. A very subtle and simple quote from this work of art awakened my senses and swiped the first layer of smog off my third eye. *"No man knows what he can do, until he tries."* Dear reader, to you this quote may be one of little-to-no significance, but to me, it traveled to a place within my mind I hadn't yet accessed. I realized I did not have a true idea of my own power and light, because I had yet to try anything outside of a sport. Sure, I compiled a strong semester once, and there were a handful of classes I excelled in, but all of that looped back to basketball, not my personal growth and development. Miseducation encouraged me to understand that education is more than what you are taught in between the four walls of a classroom. It is what you feed yourself throughout your life. Until this point, I had not given myself much of anything with sufficient substance to sustain me through my years. One of the most potent quotes from this piece of literature sharpened my perspective in a way that has not been altered since the moment I opened the book. *"If you can control a man's thinking, you do not have to worry about his action. When you determine what a man shall think, you do not have to concern yourself about what he will do. If you make a man feel that he is inferior, you do not have to compel him to accept an inferior status, for he will seek it himself. If you make a man think that he is justly an outcast, you do not have to order him to the back door. He will go without being told; and if there is no back door, his very nature will demand one."* It is critical to understand this quote, its meaning, and how it related to my life.

Miseducation was released in 1933, during the continual period of racial inequality spanning across every aspect of minority life and the judicial disparity in the federal, state, and local infrastructures in the United States of America. During this time period, segregation was legal, and this included the school systems. There was an incredible discrepancy in the funding and resources of African American schools. What was supposed to be a basic right for all American people was intentionally sabotaged for African Americans. Why? Knowledge breeds hope, knowledge breeds new life, and knowledge continues to push an effort for true equality. Inclusion feels like oppression to individuals who built a system based on their prosperity, rather than true American morals and values. It was a conscious effort during this time period to disparage the African American people to the point that some of us accepted demeaning views and actions. From 1933 to 2013 the times changed, the methods changed, the system changed, but the intent remained the same.

Before I ever stepped a toe on Limestone College's campus, and before I ever picked up a pen to complete an assignment, I was already perceived—consciously or subconsciously—as a physically superior being, with the natural characteristics necessary to be a successful collegiate athlete, but lacking the intellectual compacity to be a successful academic prospect. These stereotypes were not unbeknownst to me, growing up playing the game of basketball in predominately white areas. I always recalled individuals telling me how their daughter or son was being courted by Ivy League Universities after I relayed to them who was in my recruiting circle or my predominately black, team defeating, affluent AAU teams, or private high schools and parents reassuring their children that this game "will not be the highlight of your life." The stereotype was something that I lived with for so long, I began to wear it. As illustrated in the above quote, I felt inferior intellectually and adapted the non-caring, prideful attitude to shield the fact that I was afraid of trying, failing, and being exactly who the outside force already thought I was.

Accepting the fact that I fell into the harmful cycle of African American perception was the first step in being able to recover and rewrite my life. I was at rock bottom. I could not sink any lower than I already was during this time period, so I had no choice but to turn my eyes towards the light God revealed to me through this literature and reclaim my experience as a student and a student only. I first started by writing an essay to Limestone's board of administrators, explaining to them why my 2013 spring semester was so poor. As I was writing, I allowed myself to open my heart and let those emotions guide my pen. I took accountability for the position I placed myself in, and the mindset I'd developed by pushing everything that did not relate to basketball to the back burner. Basketball was supposed to be an accessory in my life, not a necessity of my worth. I do not make excuses about the rigorous and demanding schedule of college athletics, though such excuses could be made. In this moment, that argument was irrelevant as I only desired to return to college to resume my studies. I made it a point for these individuals to know that there was no 'next time' for me. My only option was to move forward as a student, and I was ready to receive everything I recused myself from over the past four years.

A couple weeks pass before I received a response from the college. Some days were longer than others, and it was an indication that this road to self-discovery was going to be a long and challenging one. It was easy to worry and become pessimistic when the present looked bleak and the immediate future was going to be decided by a few individuals who did not truly understand the direction your life was heading. But, I remembered that faith did not mean the road would be easy, but it made all things possible. My life was still in God's hands, and all I had to do was put my trust in His will and everything would prove to be for the betterment of me.

When I received the response from Limestone, I was hesitant to open the letter. Although I was rebuilding my spiritually and my faith, being suspended from school would affect new found hope and put my rebuilding to the ultimate test. I took a deep breath as I opened the envelope and read the letter. I skimmed through the first sections until I got to the last paragraph that stated I had been removed from academic suspension and was allowed to return to Limestone College in the fall semester of 2013 on special provisions. A new enthusiasm sprang through my body, and it was a weirdly surprising feeling. For the first time in my life, I was happy and excited about something outside of my sport.

I was not concerned about the provisions that the school had placed upon me, because a different fire had been lit inside me that I had never experienced before—the will to take every ounce of knowledge denied from my ancestors and every ounce of knowledge that I owed myself. In the coming weeks, I prepared myself for my return to Limestone College as a student. I was unaffected by what the students and faculty may or may not think about me being a fifth-year senior. I now took pride in knowing that I made a decision that was going to have an everlasting impact on my life. I spoke with my academic advisor on several occasions before selecting my classes to ensure I had a complete plan of action. With the help of my tribe and my mother, I was able to set up an apartment very close to campus, so I had access to the library and other resources I would need throughout the year.

I was taking Maria the athlete and altering her into Maria the student and intellectual. I knew the road that lied before me was full of tribulation and obstacles, but my bible said, in Deuteronomy 31:6, "***Be strong and courageous, do not***

be afraid, nor be scared of them: for the LORD your God is he who is going with you; he will not leave you nor forsake you." I was ready to seize this second chance—a second chance at school, a second chance as Maria, and a second chance at life.

12

Restoration

My fifth and final year at Limestone proved to be one of redemption and transition, officially leaving my playing career and professional aspirations in the past. I was in a place where I was okay with never picking up a basketball again, and it was oddly satisfying. After nearly two decades of dedicating my life to that game, I was ready to create new opportunities and accomplish new goals. I discovered a newfound optimism of what I could achieve, and I was ready to start living up to my potential. I had the mistakes and experiences of my past to use as a compass, preventing me from traveling a previous path, but unlike my initial integration into college, I was prepared for what lie ahead of me.

Months of idle time during the summer, thinking about my future and the road I wanted my life to take, taught me how to use and manage my time wisely, but it was still a huge adjustment in the beginning. As an athlete, I had class from 9am to 1pm, lunch with my team, weight training, practice, dinner with the team, and study hall. I was constantly required to fulfill an athletic obligation and this schedule dominated the majority of my days. The pace of my life slowed to steady, rhythmic tempo—a far cry from the overloaded, hectic stride of previous years. Although I now had ample time to complete my assignments and study, I was still left with a lot of idle time on my hands, and I did not know what to do with it. I took a team managing position with the basketball team to fill some of this gap while I continued to rehab from my surgery. The position requirements were not vigorous, and I was not under any restrictions. So, the flexibility never interfered with my studies, while still keeping me in a system of structure.

Over half of my class load in the fall of 2013 were ones I had to retake. Some were simple freshman courses that I chuckled at myself for failing in the first place, and others were classes that presented a challenge. But, instead of not attempting to do my best, and telling myself that I would not do well, convincing myself to settle for the least I could give. Instead of disregarding the class, at this juncture, I sought help and set up meetings with tutors to help me develop new tactics and different ways of understanding the material. Previously, the thought of asking for help would have embarrassed me—receiving assistance was not suitable for my "Shiloh" persona—but now, I recognized that it was merely a tool to equip me in where I was going.

Academically, I was succeeding in ways I never saw possible. However, another area of my life was not progressing as smoothly. My improvement as a student did not obliterate the occasions I felt like I was wandering in the dark. I was still having bouts of loneliness and sadness, but could not figure out why. Things were beginning to point upward for me, so why could I not be genuinely happy? I desired to reconnect with all my former teammates, but hesitated on the thought because I felt it could be detrimental to both parties. I could not be a better friend or sister until I became a better me. While I had made massive strides over the previous months, I accepted that I had to discover more about myself and what I desired. Strength and dedication to my self-healing and self-care would be essential to working through my layers of insecurity, anxiety, and armory. In order for me to do this, I first had to discover the root—or as my great grandmother would say, the "rut"—to these feelings. I realized that there was a depth to these questions that I could not answer or maneuver on my own, so I searched for help and met with a therapist on campus.

In our very first meeting, it was evident that I was extremely uneasy. I began to question my decision to receive help in this way. I thought to myself, "Maybe you really are crazy," because who voluntarily seeks therapy? As the session began, the therapist started by asking very basic and general questions, hoping to gain insight into who I was. After several minutes of primary conversation, she presents me with one last basic question. She asked me if I was "okay." I gave her a puzzled look and answered timidly, "Yeah, I guess, yes. Yes, I am okay." Her next words allowed me to drop my guard and become comfortable sharing what struggles I found myself in.

She said, "In any process of healing, you must first realize that it is okay to not be okay. True healing will not find you if you do not acknowledge all of what you feel." My stomach began to churn as a tornado of emotion took effect.

Not knowing where to start, I told her, "I am here because I am on a journey to build my life after basketball and walk in the authenticity of who I am. The problem is, I am not sure if I know who that is."

As the first session moved forward, I realized that we had not spoken about anything related to basketball or athletics. As we conversed, we spoke about hidden interests and endeavors I wanted to strive for—my passion for African American History. Until this day, I'd never verbalized my desires to my teachers, coach, or to anyone, as my life revolved around what happened in between ninety-four feet of hardwood. Expressing these aspirations to another individual, and no longer keeping what made me unique close to my chest, was refreshing, as it unlocked a box within my heart. We agree to meet bi-weekly over the next three months, and it is made clear to me that each session would be a little different—some proving to be more difficult than others, but each another stepping stone in assisting me in finding my true self and build stability that would sustain me for years to come.

Leaving this session, I was convinced that I made the right decision for my overall well-being. It did not mean I was "crazy." It meant I was courageous enough to take a proper step towards becoming the best version of myself I could be by asking for the help I desperately needed. Clarity was beginning to find me where I sought it.

It is an unfortunate stigma that exists throughout our community. That succumbing to any type of depression or mental and emotional obstacle is viewed as being "weak." We fail to understand the importance of mental health and triggers we all have. Spiritually, faith and prayer will always remain an important source of healing, but sometimes seeking a professional outlet—even if it is to simply verbalize what you feel—is needed as well. There is no shame in using the available resources necessary to practice self-care. The negative connotations placed on mental health is a stigma I refuse to wear in this moment, and I advise others to reject that idea as well.

After the first few sessions, the questions became tougher to answer and the conversations became raw and passionate. I was forced to come to terms with why I was so emotionally reserved and unavailable to so many people. Articulating my insecurities was extremely hard to accept. It was hard for me to acknowledge that I did not always feel worthy. It was hard to acknowledge that I did not always like what I saw when I looked in the mirror, and rather than expose someone to that, I shielded my "flaws" with different defense mechanisms. It was hard to acknowledge that my lack of a relationship with my father affected me a lot more than I wanted it to—more than I wanted to admit. I did not always feel worthy because the majority of the praise I heard from everyone growing up—nine times out of ten—had everything to do with my athletic ability and nothing to do with me as an individual. The pedestal I stood upon was not one of substance, but one of feelings that could easily change with one bad performance.

The fragility of my security in my beauty, intellect, and image directly related to me insulating my 'black girl' magic in more ways than one. When jokes were made about my gums and skin complexion, I laughed with the assailants to be cooler, rather than be frowned upon for not enjoying a game of "the dozens." The laughter masked the pain and glass haze my eyes would form after several minutes of jokes being exchanged. My choice of wardrobe was not off limits for some of my classmates each day. My mother made sure I had new clothes and shoes as often as she could, but I was never a "prissy" girl. Feminine, but you had to pull my teeth to put me in a dress. Constant statements of, "You need to dress more like a girl" or, "Why don't you wear makeup?" and, "Girls don't talk like that," created an atmosphere where I was never quite comfortable or allowed to be me.

I got the most attention when our team had to dress up for our basketball games, school dances, and most certainly prom. Men that barely said three words to me otherwise suddenly wanted my undivided attention. What was the biggest difference? Oh, because I wore a dress, short shorts, or a skirt that showed my curves rather than Bermuda shorts, capris, and actual blue jeans with no holes in them. Why did it take me having to step out of myself for you to notice that there is an actual individual that exists here? These were thoughts and questions I chose not to engage in. To defend myself, I agreed with the negativity being said about me, or beat an individual to the punch and expressed it before they could, thinking I could lessen the blow if I said it first. Not realizing that I was picking up their negative perception and wearing it for them.

The biggest challenge for me was coming to terms with the emotional pain and bitterness I harbored for not having a great relationship with my father. As I got older, I relayed the same message to myself; that I was going to be fine, and I did not need him for anything. Word from the wise: no matter how much time has passed and no matter what age you are, the lack of a relationship with a parent is an emptiness that is never filled. Yes, you can develop ways of dealing with it or suppressing the hurt and anger you feel from it, but to live with this, you must be able to forgive and learn how to accept the apology that you may never get to hear. The interesting part of that sentence is, that is advice I have not been able to apply to myself just yet. However, I am finally in a place to say that I would like to.

The first step to begin healing was acknowledging the ways that this minimal relationship molded me into the young woman I became. Everything inside me was guarded and I questioned everyone's true intentions, as I believed every person I encountered had an underline. I was bitter when I saw my teammates who came from two-parent households—their dad being the first one they hugged or logging onto social media and seeing pictures of them with their fathers with the caption: "Daddy's girl." The bitterness stemmed from me feeling like I missed out on something that was supposed to be special, and his failure to acknowledge his role in why our relationship suffered. To this day, my relationship with my father continues to test my patience and travels along a road of uneasy uncertainty. I have not found a way to surrender the past, because there are so many unanswered questions. Yes, my life turned out great. I was raised by a magnificent single mother, with the assistance of an incredible tribe. I just simply wonder how different things would have been had there been two number one fans in my life.

During a particular session, my therapist presented a question to me that I did not have an answer for. She asked, "Why do you categorize your friends?" When she posed this question, I looked at her confused until I gathered what she was asking. As I have illustrated throughout this piece of work, I call my childhood friends my "tribe" and my teammates my "crew." Subconsciously, I separated my friends by the length of time I have known them, not by the significance they held in my life, even though it does not read that way to them or me. This question opened new insight into my friendships, as I began to explore why. Never calling the individuals I met in college my tribe was a way of protecting myself and keeping them at a safe distance. Refer to chapter two where I describe what "tribe" means to me and the importance it holds. That was the pinnacle in my personal life. By calling these individuals "crew," it was to illustrate to them that they were very important people in my life, but it also showed them that they were not top tier in my life either.

A friend is a friend, no matter how long you have or have not known them. If they consistently display the qualities of love, loyalty, trustworthiness, and optimism, they are your tribe and deserve to be treated as such. Categories devalue the blossoming of new friendships and possibilities, making it hard to understand the true importance of what your friends are bringing to your life. Discovering this truth assisted me in being able to rebuild some friendships with some of my tribe at Limestone. These sessions had become a time I looked forward to. Not only was I developing heathy ways to sort through everything that had shackled me, but I was starting to allow the light of Maria to shine through and be content in all that she is.

I formed a routine each day to continue onward in my spiritual, mental, and emotional rebuilding. From the first moment I rise in the morning, I spend time reading and meditating on my bible verse of the day. I've discovered that thanking God for my awakening each morning and spending time in His word provides me with a fierce energy to jumpstart my day. I went to my classes on campus and spent an hour or two in the library studying and working on my homework for the week, before or after assisting with practices. Lastly, I read powerful pieces of African American literature that intrigued me more and more each time I read them. It was something compelling about learning the obstacles we faced historically, the pioneers of our people, and the events that were not only withheld from my classrooms, but also how these instances shaped American history.

W.E.B Dubois is one of my favorite African American intellects in the span of our history. I was introduced to him in high school by an American History teacher, who was a rare commodity in life. This particular teacher taught this subject genuinely. It struck me how she never sanitized the horrors and tragedies of American history. She always taught me how to read between the lines of amendments, legislations, and government acts, especially when it pertained to African Americans. To this day, this teacher and I remain close, and her teachings never influenced me more than they did during this time in my life. She presented me with Dr. Dubois, as she knew his accomplishment as the first African American to receive his doctorate from Harvard, his messages, and ideas would attract me. It was something extraordinary about his demand for civil rights and political opportunities for African Americans and the conviction that equality was never to be compromised. I read his book "The Souls of Black Folk" during my final year at Limestone and traveled back to those high school teachings while opening new perspectives.

Dr. Dubois stated the: *"Negro is a sort of seventh son, born with a veil, and gifted with second-sight in this American world, a world which yields him no true self-consciousness, but only lets him see himself through the revelation of the other world. It is a peculiar sensation, this double-consciousness, this sense of always looking at one's self through the eyes of others, of measuring one's soul by the tape of a world that looks on in amused contempt and pity. One ever feels his twoness, an American, a Negro, two souls, two thoughts, two unreconciled strivings, two warring ideals in one dark body, whose dogged strength alone keeps it from being torn asunder."*

Before reading the following sentences please take the time to re-read that quote. Part of what makes learning African American history exceptional, but equally eerie, is the ability to read a passage of literature that was written in 1903 and still be able to apply parts of it to your modern life. That is a very perplexing fact, because it can feel like a double-edged sword; on one side you are excited to be exposed to your culture and knowledge of self, but on the other side, learning this history equips you to be able to see that the perception and intent of our society has not changed. Upon arriving in this country, everything that made us human and an individual was stripped from us and replaced with the identity other people created for us. Never being allowed to stand firm in our own identities.

The power of this lies in our ability to persevere despite

unspeakable social, economic, and political odds. What made this passage relatable for me was the fact that I had been living behind the veil of characteristics and expectations that were forced upon me from the day I picked up a basketball. I saw examples of the "stereotypical black athlete." Just because I was an athlete, does not mean that is all I wanted for my life. My love for the game was supposed to provide me with a free education and serve as a launching pad to greater opportunities. I heard from the masses what they expected me to be, and it was never a doctor, lawyer, professor, and so on. So, I used that as my shield. Each African American in this country, no matter their status, has hidden behind a veil of some compacity. In 2013—now in 2017—as in 1903, veils still exist. Discovering this fact was the first chain link released from around my brain.

One day, as I was leaving campus, I ran into a young brother who was on a tour of our facilities. This young brother left the group to walk over and greet me. As he was walking towards me, I was able to recognize who he was. During my sophomore year, a local teacher—who was married to a faculty member at Limestone—would bring a young student of hers to all our home games. After each game, he made it a point to tell me how much he loved watching me play, and how I was his favorite player on the team. This young man was now in high school—and having held me on such a high pedestal—he was confused as to why I was in Gaffney, South Carolina, still attending Limestone College. From his expectation, I was supposed to be across the Atlantic Ocean playing basketball professionally. To my surprise I was not agitated by his questions or ashamed to be viewed as someone who "didn't make it." This, in itself, was indication of where I was in my life and how comfortable I was with that chapter being closed. I explained to this young man that it was not in God's plan for me to play overseas, and that my sole focus now was to finish getting my degree.

His response was, "I feel you. I still want to be like you when I go to college." I jerked my head towards him as if I had heard my favorite Sam Cooke record scratch. I know he was referring to my basketball ability, as he was an athlete himself, but the horror of any young brother and sister going through the raging waters I was currently swimming out of terrified me. Before this moment, I'd never stopped to consider the next generation of student athletes who were looking at me as a source of guidance and inspiration. Up until a few months ago, I had not given them anything to aspire to that would bolster them through their lives. I honed my attention on this young man before speaking.

"I am a fifth-year senior because I did not see the value in my education until I almost lost everything. It took me losing basketball to understand that life is much grander than what I could do on a basketball court, and God extended me a second chance. If you do not remember anything else from me, remember this, never put yourself in a position to need a second chance." He hung onto my every word like it was the gospel, and I know he heard me with his heart. I extend my contact information to him and make myself available if he needs assistance with anything in his life moving forward.

I know the advice I gave him is something he will remember, even if he did not fully understand it in the moment. This young brother will never be able to fully understand what he did for me that day. I committed to investing in a young life for the first time, and it was overwhelmingly fulfilling. God placed him in my path to assist me in discovering my purpose. I used my failings and shortcomings to equip a member of the next generation. It dawned on me that I could have the same, if not a bigger, impact on people's lives than I did when I held a basketball in my hand. The mistakes and pain of my previous years had now become beneficial. Shortly after this exchange, I contacted the local boys and girls club to inquire about volunteer opportunities to visit with their kids and contribute to after school tutoring sessions. I was now aware of the platform God gifted me, and how I was supposed to use it. What I represented to these young brothers and sisters was bigger than any game.

After the fall semester, the lowest grade I received in my classes was a C in Biology. After all the studying and tutoring sessions, that was a class that I just did not gel with. I was not happy about that C, but I was satisfied with the effort I expended. I was genuinely proud of myself and the progress I'd made. Five months ago, I could not have envisioned myself being in this space. Before going home for Christmas break, I met with my advisor, who informed there was a possibility that I could graduate in the spring of 2014, but he would have to approve an overload on my schedule. He decided against it. He believed that my current hours were the proper pace for me, evident by the semester I had. I agreed with him, as I wanted to stay on this course of success. Not approving an overload left me with two additional courses to be taken in the summer months with my requirements being completed by July. This made me eligible for our December graduation.

Returning to Limestone for my last semester, I grew increasingly distant from basketball. I stopped showing up to the practices as often and stopped coming to the gym to visit. Knowing that I was mere months away from completing the requirements for my degree, motivated me in ways I had not experienced before. But again, too much idle time was becoming my enemy. I applied for a part-time position at the local Nike outlet—working twenty to twenty-five hours a week. A few weeks later, I was hired as a new "athlete." Yes, I wanted this job, but integrating an establishment where I did not know a soul was very nerve wracking and put me to the test. Number one, if you are going to work in retail, you must carry certain pleasantries when you meet customers, as it is your job to make them feel comfortable enough to purchase your product. Number two, entering a situation where I did not have the comfort of familiarity was uncharted territory, and I was anxious to see how I would navigate this terrain.

I was extremely quiet the first few staff meetings and training sessions—not standoffish, but observant as I tried to read where and how I could fit in. Fortunately, my co-workers were magnificent people. So, when I stepped out of my comfort zone and initiated conversations, I was made to feel right at home. Being conscious of my nervousness and my shyness, allowed me to control it and take a shot at being open, which ended up developing friendships that I still maintain to this day. I was excited about arriving to work when I was on the schedule—not so much for the job, but for the people. Being able to fellowship, laugh, and revel in the delight of new connections, we shared incalculable moments before, after, and outside of our job. The "friend" connections I was making, seamlessly became tribe connections. My life took on a refreshing rebirth, not only has new bonds formed, but as old ones resurfaced. I was in consistent contact with former teammates and spent a lot of time with the ones that were closest to the city. I tried a different approach in my appreciation for them, sending random texts to "show love" and check in on how they and their loved ones were doing. I rejoiced in gratitude knowing that these kinships were still firm and only growing as we all matured.

Unlike the May 2013 graduation, when the May of 2014 graduation ceremony arrived, I was not in emotional shambles, but cheerful for my fellow students. I was even cheerful for myself, knowing that only two classes stood in the way of achieving the same unforgettable feeling. My final classes were two repeats, and two classes that, even with extra help, I still found challenging. The exams for both classes were 25% to 30% of my overall grade. I deliberately made sure that my daily assignments were above standard, as the quizzes and tests in these courses presented a constant obstacle. As the exam day approached, I ceased all activities outside of my studies—except the time I was scheduled to work. However, I requested to work minimum hours, so I could have more time to prepare myself. My tribe understood why I chose to stay home versus go to a bar or another outing. Years ago, I would have left my books and responsibilities on the shelf for a few hours of turn-up, but now, my future was at stake. Although I was doing everything humanly possible to study for these exams, I was fearful. Being this close to an accomplishment that was going to change my life, and something that had looked unachievable a year ago, frightened me. Instead of retreating, I expressed these thoughts and concerns to my mother and my friends, who again, reminded me that God was in control and I had nothing to worry about. This was my time to seize.

I took my exams in the coming days. I have never prayed harder over anything in my life. I receive an A and a B on my exams, but I had to wait three agonizing days until my professors informed me of what my final grades would be. I emailed them every day during this span, and each day their responses grew increasingly annoyed. I wasn't bothered in the least. During these three days, I found it hard to relax or concentrate on anything other than finding out what my grades were. My tribe tried to distract me and drag me out of my apartment to ease my mind, but nothing worked. Serenity would not find me until I heard from my professors.

On day four, my phone rang and I answered as soon as I saw it was a Limestone College number. I deeply exhaled as my hands began to shake. On the other end was one of my professors, who informed me that my final grade in his class was a B. I smiled brightly, relieved, but I still had one more grade to wait on. I checked my student portal upon returning home and saw that I'd received an A in my final class at Limestone

College. After reading my final grades, I immediately called my mother, and as soon as she answered the phone, I cried tears of persistence and joy. I kept repeating, "I did it, I did it, I really did it!" My mother began to cry with me as I struggled to speak through my tears. To be able to say that I had a college degree was surreal. A year prior, I found myself in the grip of darkness and self-doubt, on the verge of giving up on life. And, here I stood now, achieving an accomplishment that for so long I never believed I could. God and my tribe did not allow me to give up, and I discovered the power, strength, and intelligence of my being. Overcoming my failures and short-comings, along with society's doubts of what I had the capability to do, was validation for everything I discovered over the past year at Limestone. In hindsight, do I wish I had been a better decision maker in my life? Yes, but I do not have any re-grets. All the pain, struggles, hard work, and long hours were worth the moment I completed my degree. The elation moving through my body in that moment surpassed anything I'd accomplished as an athlete. This degree could not be dimin-ished or debated, and I stood on the shoulders of my ancestors whose fight and spirit allowed me to celebrate this moment. My mind was awakened, my eyes were open, and I felt as if God gave me new life without the shackles of false securities. In this fifth year, at twenty-two years old, I finally discovered Maria. I discovered my true influence, potential, and belief in myself. I was already equipped to be great, but like so many athletes, I didn't even know it.

13

Graduation Part 2

The morning of my Limestone graduation, I woke up full of excitement and a little anxiety. As I lay in my bed, I reflected over the past five years and was astounded by the progress I had made in my life. For so long, this day felt like a fleeting illusion, slipping through the pads of my fingertips. I traveled and conquered the troubled waters of self-doubt, negative internalization, and a lack of identity. I knew that me being in this position was nothing but God's grace, guidance, and mercy. I struggled to understand why He blessed me with the opportunity to change my life after traveling so far from Him for so long, but I do not seek my own understanding; I simply show my gratitude.

My mother entered my room, surprised to find me awake. When we locked eyes, she flashed the biggest Kool-Aid smile, as she started to execute my uncle's neighborhood famous "Stick Man" dance. We shared a gut-wrenching laugh, and she expressed how much she loves me and how proud of me she is. Before she exited my room, she screamed,

"We gon' have a celebrate!" After hearing that line from one of Tyler Perry's films, my mother had been waiting for the perfect time to scream it, and this was definitely a celebratory moment.

I got up and got dressed for the day. My mother and I were leaving a few hours, before the rest of my family, because she had scheduled me a hair appointment in the neighboring town of Spartanburg. My tribe had traveled from far and wide to commemorate this occasion. Each of them spent countless hours planning my graduation and preparing for me to walk across that stage. I wished I had more time to spend with them this morning, but South Carolina awaited.

While driving to Spartanburg, my mother and I had the time of our lives, holding our own version of carpool karaoke, singing the soulful tunes of the Motown classics. I had never seen my mother more cheerful, and I knew she felt a sense of relief and accomplishment being the single mother of two children with college degrees. When we arrived at the hair salon, I was congratulated by all the stylists and other customers. Over the past five years, this salon represented a piece of home. A place that was ours, where black women could come to relax, catch up on the town gossip, and be given a reality check. This was a place of camaraderie, and most importantly, fellowship. These women watched me grow from an eighteen-year-old child to at twenty-three-year-old young adult. Their numerous conversations about our community, politics, religion, television shows, films, and relationships were a constant reminder of how special it is to be a black woman. This shop played an important role in me being comfortable in my blackness, so it was only fitting that this be my first stop on such a special day. As always, the conversation was memorable. As I departed from these wonderful ladies, I felt a tug at my heartstrings, but I assured them that this was 'see you later', never goodbye.

During graduation rehearsal, I felt flutters of butter-flies in my stomach, but the magnitude of the moment has not struck me yet. Since the majority of my fifth-year classes were online, I graduated with the extended campus program. As I observed everyone around me, I noticed that there were a lot of individuals who looked like me. I was surrounded by hundreds of brothers and sisters who also embarked on a journey of achievement and higher education. It was a calming feeling, being able to witness and share this moment with my people.

After practice, everyone dispersed into their corners and various parts of the campus to get dressed for the ceremony. Members of my tribe, including some very close Shiloh family friends, now joined my mother. The seating was first come, first served, but in true Shiloh fashion, my tribe roped off an entire row specifically for them and other family members yet to arrive. It was safe to assume that the administration wanted to tell my family they should not rope (yes rope) an entire section off, as it would inconvenience other parties, but when my grandmother is quick to remind you that she is "Judge Harrell's widow!" it's probably not a good idea.

I got dressed and lined up with my fellow graduates in the campus library. I took the time to converse with some of these graduates. Since I was walking with the extended campus, there were people from different parts of North and South Carolina, as well as different age groups. One particular person was a black woman from Columbia, South Carolina, who was in her early forties. She was proud to share that with us. She told us that she had her children at a young age and once they got, "good and grown" there was no excuse she could use to justify her not receiving her college degree. This was a breathtaking experience for me; not only this woman's determination, but hearing others share their stories of perseverance and about the barriers they had to overcome to arrive at this moment. It was impossible to escape the significance of this moment. Each person spoke about becoming teachers, professors, journalists, engineers, or lawyers. The amount of black excellence in that library was staggering, and I was proud to know that this was the stock in which I came from. We shared playful and light-hearted moments with each other, as if we had known each other for a few years instead of a few hours. There is a spirit and a rhythm in the midst of black unity that can only be explained by God.

After over an hour of conversation, it was now time to walk into the auditorium. Each of us shared the sentiments of ecstatic nervousness. Some of the graduate's used humor to mask these feelings, as the suggested we "March in like the old church choir!" We busted a slight two-step down the stairs, humming the church hymn, "Hush, somebody's calling my name." As we entered the auditorium, I observed a sea of people, all standing to their feet to welcome all the graduates. The totality of this moment finally sunk in, and it was more gratifying than I could have ever imagined. I did not know what to expect because I had barely thought about this day. I had lost the belief that my degree was achievable. I saw my tribe to my right as I walked to my seat. Each one of their of faces was filled with delight and glistening eyes from unfallen tears.

Graduation commenced and the ceremony was, admittedly, a bit boring. I cannot tell you who was the keynote speaker. All I remember is an awkward attempt to charm us by referencing Beyoncé. I think everyone felt as confused as I was. All the graduates regained excitement when it was time for our names to be called and to receive our degrees. Once again, our families were instructed to hold their applause until all the graduates had been announced. I glanced at my family who looked around at each other, conveying an expression of, "I know he don't expect us to be quiet when she walks across that stage." I laughed to myself as I knew exactly what was about to happen.

I could barely contain my enthusiasm as our administrator began to read each name. With each passing second, he was getting closer to my row. I took a deep breath when we were instructed to walk to the side of the stage. I bowed my head and closed my eyes to appreciate and be present in my moment. I did not want to take any of this day for granted. The hands I stood on and the path that was forged for me by my ancestors led me to this very stage. My past did not define me, what the outside world thought about me did not define me, and I no longer lived in the stereotype of a black athlete. The moment I decided to take my life back, and the moment I valued the very knowledge that would sustain me until I take my last breath, I had already won. The blood which contained strength, diligence, self-pride, knowledge, self-love, and unity was passed down from generation to generation and was flowing through my body like the river of Jordan, pumping every measure of my heart.

I passed the administrator my name card and walked onto the stage. I noticed that the lights were extremely bright—a representation of my internal light. I focused on the president of Limestone, who was smiling back at me. My concentration was briefly interrupted when I heard a loud roar of "SHILOH" coming from my family's section. I could not contain my laughter as I shook the president's hand. We shared a moment as he expressed how proud he was of me for "sticking with it." It was pleasing to know that a man of his stature and position kept an eye on my progress after my playing career ended.

I walked back to my seat and glanced at my tribe, realizing that every single person was crying. Not Denzel Washington in Glory tears, but Viola Davis in Fences tears—face scrunched, snotty tears. As electric as this moment was for me, my tribe shared in every emotion. They were there during my anguish, and were now here witnessing my breakthrough. My family's love ran so deep that each one of them wanted this moment for me almost more than I wanted it for myself. When graduation concluded, I made a B-line to my family and was greeted with plenty of hugs and kisses. Joining my family were my friends from Nike and my coaching staff. At one point, my coaches freely expressed to me that, once I left Limestone in the spring of 2013, they did not believe I would make it across that stage.

Here I was, in this moment, sharing my triumph with the individuals God used to extend this opportunity to me. It was a beautiful and pleasant reminder that no matter where life takes me, I would always have a family in Gaffney, South Carolina. Some of my former teammates were not able to make the trip, but they made sure I knew how proud I made them. We were now in various parts of the country, separated by distance, but forever bound by kinship. Becoming a Limestone College Alumni was the most memorable day of my existence—a day of personal validation and development, a day that showed me that the pain of my past was a temporary roadblock to the larger blessing upon the hill.

The following night was my graduation party in my hometown. My family had created a dream like venue to make sure this was the celebration of a lifetime. When I arrived at the destination with my friends, I entered a dimly lit room to the screams and exuberance of my family, friends, Shiloh community, former teachers, and anyone else that played a vital role in my transformation. The venue may have been different, but how we partied remained the same. The DJ played "Outstanding" by the legendary Gap Band after I made my rounds to speak to everyone. That song officially got the party started off right! DVD's of iconic Soul Train dancers were projected on the walls as we danced, and I heard shouts of, "Turn it up!" or, "Turn it off!", "Go head now!", "Don't hurt nobody!" and, "What's that lil dance y'all young folk do?" That was when I knew I was home. All of us danced into oblivion and capped the night off with our own Soul Train line to our traditional jam, "The Payback," by the one and only James Brown. This party marked the peak of an interesting chapter of my life. It was hard to believe how far I'd come and the accomplishments tagged to my name. Celebrating life, love, and fellowship with my tribe and rebuilding my basic principles prepared me for the "real world." I was ready to step out into the unknown and receive my blessings. *Guide my feet, hold my hand, Lord lead me home, and lead me into being a reflection of your grace.*

20

Unshackled

August 9th, 2014, Ferguson, Missouri: eighteen-year-old Michael Brown, an unarmed black man was shot and killed by white police officer Darren Wilson. I, like many others, watched CNN and MSNBC coverage of the immediate aftermath of this tragedy, and I was astonished by what I saw. The body of a young black man continued to lay in the Midwestern heat, in the peak of the day, as seconds, minutes, and hours passed by. I opened my twitter app and began to read countless testimonies from witnesses, reporters, children, adults, activists, educators, and concerned citizens who were horrified by the catastrophe that had just taken place. As I was watching my television and reading my social media apps, I struggled to process what I was seeing. However, I quickly realized that there were inconsistencies in what was being reported to us by the news outlets and what the people were reporting. The power of social media lies in the ability to have our own tools to decipher truths vs falsehoods and justice vs injustice.

As time continued to pass and more information—including cell phone videos—was released, it felt as if the life had been sucked out of my body. I watched the police department fail to follow their own stout protocol, releasing statements that attempted to demonize and discredit Mike Brown, some news reports, and the voice of the people. I slowly but surely grasped the realization that an unarmed black youth was murdered, with his hands up, by a man sworn to protect and serve. That fact was one that latched onto my conscience and never surrendered its hold. I began to delve into why and how this happened.

I reflected on my community's layered relationship, historically, with law enforcement and why it had been so fractured for decades. I could only comprehend the depths of a larger issue enabling Darren Wilson to kill a Mike Brown. Our history was unmodified: from Watts in 1965, to Detroit in 1967, to Watts again in 1992, to Ferguson in 2014. The cycle persists, the oppression evolves, and the tactics become hidden horrors. The bias of the criminalization upon black bodies rooted in false truths and false fears, don white robes and are handed blue badges, sheriff titles, mayor seats, city council boards, governor honors, state and federal representation, congressional prestige, Supreme Court benches, and eventually travel upward to the President of the United States. More concerning still are the individuals who stand beside these men, adamantly disagreeing with these views, but complacent in normalcy. They hesitate to lift a finger for the citizens with the boot of legalized crimes upon their necks, painting us under a broad brush of who they were taught African American's are. They lack empathy for things and people that do not directly benefit or affect them.

I now live with the information that there could be a Trayvon Martin, Michael Brown, Rekia Boyd, Oscar Grant, or Aiyana Jones across any city in America, at any time. I considered whether I had a strong enough voice to actually make a difference. *Will my conviction be met with acceptance or confusion? Do I have the necessary attributes to educate and inspire others?* With Oscar, I did not. With Aiyana, I did not. With Rekia, I did not. With Trayvon, I did not. With Mike Brown, I did, as my personal expansion continued to move at a rapid pace. My education did not cease at Limestone, and I finally equipped myself with the fundamental means to retrieve what was hidden inside me, polish it off, and stand firm in what I believed. The more I learned, the bigger and bolder the message I carried became, and in this new light of Maria, it was not a message I wanted to withhold.

September 1st, 2014: I was hired as the JV Girls Basketball coach at my alma mater, TC Roberson high school. It was my first job in the professional domain. I had not considered being a coach for very long, but this opportunity provided me with a chance to use the game to mold and teach the next generation. Upon accepting this job, I made it clear that my ideals had very little to do with basketball anymore and everything to do with instilling information in the youth that would sustain them through high school, with the encouragement to attain higher education. My basketball pedigree ultimately allowed me in the door, but I had plans of rewrapping the building.

Walking into a meeting with the varsity coach and the players, I was very nervous. Children of this generation were slightly different than I was. They deal with a different set of circumstances, pressures, and anxieties than my generation did. I worried about how I would be received by these players, as I was merely ten years older than the youngest ones. I wondered if my message was one they cared to receive or connect with. The varsity coach explained that some of these players had dealt with tough circumstances outside of school and basketball, making them "challenging to handle at times". Nonetheless, she was pleased that I was part of the staff, as she felt I would be able to connect with these players on a level she could not. Please keep the last sentence in my mind as you read further.

As I stepped to the front of the gym to address the team, my hands started to tremble and sweat. I cleared my throat to ensure there would be no embarrassing cracks in my voice and to ensure that I was heard loud and clear. Before I ever opened my mouth, I noticed that all eyes and attention were on me, ready to receive what I was about to give. I introduced myself and listed everything I had accomplished as a high school and collegiate basketball player—mouths dropped. Until that point, I'd never considered that I played on a level that the majority of these high school players were never going to experience; that in itself was an inspiration. I quickly transitioned into my real message.

"We are here to play basketball, yes, and every time you step on that court, I expect you to give me every ounce of everything you have inside of you—for yourself, and most importantly, for your teammates. Never lose sight of the fact that basketball is an extracurricular activity for a reason. It comes secondary to your education, and that education travels far beyond your classrooms and into your personal knowledge of who you are and where you come from. Wins and losses on this court do not amount to the wins and losses of life. Everything that I teach you within these ninety-four feet will prepare you for what's next." As with the young man I ran into on the campus of Limestone, these young women received each of my words with an open heart and mind. Upon the closure of the meeting, I was swarmed by my junior-varsity players, as well as the varsity participants, who were anxious to get started. They relayed their

thoughts about the upcoming season, while cracking jokes and remaining upbeat. These young ladies had no idea what they were in for.

I referred to my college routine and information to create a pre-season workout regimen for my team. It took over three weeks for my players to adjust to the intensity of my coaching style and workouts. As much as they were learning about what I expected, this was a learning experience for me as well. I figured out which players could take tough criticism, and which players needed me to be a little more conscience of my words and critiques—not because they were "soft," because certain players do not respond well if they feel like they are being torn down. I had the challenge of implementing different methods and strategies to maximize what the player could give. I was able to find a perfect balance with my team. When we stepped on the basketball court, it was time to take care of business and play to the best of our capabilities, but off the court, these young ladies brought out my playful side—which continued to grow as I spent time with them.

Once official practices and games began, we were still a bit behind the curve. My team was not overloaded with talent, but the trade-off was the girls' dedication to hard work, and it was my job to create an environment where they felt successful regardless of what happened on the basketball court. Whether it was small competition games in practice or rewards for academic achievements, it was my duty in a position of leadership to assist in building their character. During the first half of our season, we won one game. Most coaches would have taken this very hard, but the silver lining in defeat was the growth that I witnessed from game to game. These ladies learned how to come together, problem-solve, and encourage each other, even though the end result seemed bleak. They were developing life skills that would only benefit them long after they removed their TC Roberson jersey. My patience was tested at different points throughout this season, however, working with teenagers, I would have expected nothing less as I helped them adapt their skills. A few of my players started to report to class late, disrespect their teachers, and show up to practice five or ten minutes late, then have the audacity to question why I had to punish them. The blessing of once carrying a similar mindset they currently possessed, was my ability to identify their actions before they got too far. I had full understanding of where it all stemmed from. My approach was to discipline and develop. I would discipline these young ladies, through basketball, for breaking my rules, but afterwards, offered a piece of myself and my journey to expose them to what lay ahead if they continued to develop bad habits. The importance of sharing my story with them was to display that I was not a superhero that had never done anything wrong. I appreciated the high regard they gave me, but I refused to be detached from reality again.

In addition to my coaching duties, I became a substitute teacher, not only for the extra cash, but to experience what it felt like being in a classroom setting with bright and vibrant young minds. I entered a junior and senior classroom, to sub for a history teacher who left behind a very thorough and detailed lesson plan. As I read, I saw that the class was working on the civil rights era, studying the significance of the life of Dr. Martin Luther King and his works. I did not have to stand at the board much, as majority of her plan included reading the chapters and completing worksheet packets. As the students walked into class, they smiled and I figured they knew who I was based off of my players boasting, and as a young woman later told me, "Google." As the class began working, I walked to each student and asked if they were okay, offering help when needed.

The majority of them objected until I approached the desk of a young black boy who displayed a look of confusion. I noticed he had not completed much of his work. As I sat down and questioned him, he told me he was having a hard time concentrating because there were things that he didn't understand. Initially, I thought he was referring to his work. He expressed that he was speaking about Tamir Rice—a twelve-year-old child killed by law enforcement in Cleveland, Ohio after the police thought the young boy had a firearm. My heart dropped as this young brother expressed his thoughts and concerns with me. My mind scrambled as I tried to think of what to say to a seventeen-year-old black boy to ease his fear and comfort his concerns.

I had nothing philosophical to say, so I let my heart take over. *"Unfortunately, we live in a society where our kids have to grow up quick and deal with a system that demonizes and offers minimal protection, for me or you, and anyone who looks like us. Tamir was the victim of a legal system that told him he did not matter. If you have not heard it already, someone will tell you that you don't either, but it is important to remember to NEVER accept what someone else thinks about you. Prepare yourself to conquer your dreams. Mourn for Tamir, but also live for Tamir, and its starts right here in this classroom."* The young man smiled and thanked me before resuming his reading. I felt a sense of pride when I walked away from him, because I had just given him some encouragement when he was in need. There were no words I could have said to completely erase his pain or his fear; everything this student felt was valid, and I thank God that He used me to reach this young man on that day.

It was satisfying being able to build relationships with

these students, offer a helping hand or striking up a conversation based on things of interest. Some students that I was told to "beware" of were the students that gave me the least amount of trouble. I invested a small fraction of my time to them to share my experiences and offer the knowledge of self. Just showing a child that I cared enough to spend a few minutes with him or her was something that was cherished, and this continued to pull me further into my purpose. Being a substitute teacher illustrated the type of influence an educator has and that influence can venture well beyond the four walls of a classroom. Educators have the power to plant seeds in our young people, with the hope they will be cultivated later in their lives. For the first time since I stepped off a basketball court, I felt that I belonged, and I began to consider the possibilities of a teaching career.

Mid-way through the basketball season, my team finally scored a few wins and started playing the best basketball they had played all season, but I became disconnected from my overall environment. As time progressed, I began to feel a discord with the varsity coaching staff for a number of reasons. As with our JV team, the varsity squad had their own set of challenges to overcome on the basketball court. Being the head coach of the girls' basketball team at TC Roberson brought an immense amount of pressure because the school had a rich tradition of winning, and when it wasn't happening, the environment became uneasy—which easily allowed me to question my own effectiveness. This matter, along with the natural gravitation of the varsity players to my presence, and my refusal to conform to how other coaches thought I should do things, created a wedge between the two parties.

The very thing I was praised for in my initial meeting— being able to connect with the players on a level the other coaches could not—was now viewed as a detriment, as insecure feelings about conversations I had with students clouded judgment. Because of my position as a JV coach, I was viewed as an individual with less stature, instead of someone who held a basketball pedigree that could be beneficial. I rebelled against being told what offenses I should run and how I should manage my team. They questioned why I did not practice the day before a game, and were unsatisfied with my request to not hold any athletic events on Dr. Martin Luther King Jr's national holiday—as I had instructed my players to go and participate in the city's annual prayer service and Dr. King March through downtown Asheville. You may be thinking, "As a first year coach, you should have been open to advice." My dear reader, there is a difference between someone offering authentic guidance and someone with an underlying agenda attached to a memo of knowing my place.

Being firm in my belief in myself, and my ability, I did not fully understanding how to navigate the professional landscape as a black woman yet. I became passive aggressive, trying to avoid confrontation, but never surrendering my ideas of what I wanted. I held several conversations with my mother about how I felt I was being treated, and her advice was to stay the course and think about the players who needed me, to use them as my motivation to keep coming back. By the time the season had ended, my fellow coaches and I were not speaking to each other, and it forced players and parents from both teams to inadvertently choose sides. I faced a real decision about my future as a coach at my alma mater heading into the off season. My first instinct was to hand in my resignation because I did not want to be part of the program any longer. Every time I went to take that step, I thought about my players, the relationships we had built, and how they depended on me every day. So, I backed out of that decision.

Near the conclusion of the season, I got a phone call from the local newspaper. A reporter wanted to write a story about my successes, and why I came back home to coach high school basketball. I happily accepted, as I had never been extended the opportunity to speak about where I came from. I knew it would a broader audience insight into who I am and hoped to become. While being interviewed, I noticed that I was surprisingly comfortable sharing personal information with a stranger. I held no reservations about verbalizing my experiences, my faith, my transformation, and my interests. I was anxious to read the article, and excited about what the city would be able to learn from me... until I read the final published piece. Joy disintegrated in the coming days as I fully processed what happened. The article was a far cry from the information I shared and painted me as a gutter kid who survived the despicable Shiloh community. I was called a "survivor" of a single parent home who used basketball as a "ticket to a better life," not as a chance to get a free education, which would serve as a pathway to endless opportunities. The optics of this article alarmed me as my family, my community, and I were presented as something we were not.

The most disturbing instance within this article was the altering and exclusion of my statements. Speaking on my community, I'd originally stated, "You do not hear a lot of the positives that come out of Shiloh." This statement was altered to, "There are not a lot of positives that come out of Shiloh," which completely changed the meaning of my statement. The intent was to share my accomplishments and show the next generation how to strive, while maintaining pride for where you came from. The altering of my thoughts presented an idea that I prospered *despite* my community, and that hurt me deeply. Words of my faith and God's grace sustaining me through a difficult time in my life were completely excluded altogether. In the end, the article was not a true representation of who I was or of my journey to who I am becoming.

This article was the reporter's interpretation of my neighborhood and who he thought I was coming from that area of town. This reporter attempted to reinforce the stereotype I had struggled to get out from under my entire life. My education and athletic ability were never mentioned in the same sentence, nor was my college graduation highlighted. Basketball, through his eyes, was my only opportunity to make something of my life; and once my injury occurred, I had no choice but to return home and coach. This reporter failed to remove his bias and open his beliefs to true narrative. The article empowered his label, while undermining my accomplishments. I was angered not only by this careless and poorly written article, but also at myself for satisfying the falsehoods of society's picture of black athletes.

Additionally, it was critical to understand the misconception of Shiloh and black communities that are similar in stature. Outwardly, people who have never visited my neighborhood believe the worst of it, because God forbid African Americans live in various communities; it must be a low income, crime ridden area. They all must be the same, right? WRONG. What people do not like to share is the rich historical legacy of Shiloh and the individuals who occupy it, who hold some of the most important jobs in the city—the sense of pride and community that enables you to walk outside your home and still feel safe, spend countless hours on "The Strip," and participate in any community event someone has planned. Holding an open invitation to anyone's cookout or get together you pass by in the neighborhood and looking out for your fellow brother or sister because you are bound by the ties of S.H.I.L.O.H. We are not a community without faults, but we are one of resilience and dignity. So, we will not wear the labels you force upon us, and we will not cower in the fight to preserve all we have always been. Shiloh versus everybody. This experience taught me a valuable lesson in being mindful of who I choose to share my story with. Research offered me answers into this reporter's reputation, and his conflicts with other black athletes who emerged from my city. Life in the real world was teaching me at a rapid pace, but each experience came complete with its own blessing.

The tumultuous basketball season, in addition to this article—which, despite my discontent, was received well by others—proved to be the final straw for me being a part of the TC Roberson basketball program. I was unhappy and troubled about the decision. I was now thrust into thinking about what I was going to do next. I had to break the news to my players and their parents at the end of the season banquet. As I explained to them that I was moving on, I became emotional when I observed the faces of my team—some were very sad, others began to shed tears. I invested in them, and in return, they believed in me and believed in what I could do for them. They discovered a side of me that I lacked awareness of. I made it a point to reiterate that no matter where God placed me, no matter how much time may pass before I saw them again, I was a mere phone call away and would forever be at their service. The only thing changing was my title.

In hindsight, my exiting the program made perfect sense. Although I still had a problem with how I was treated, to run an effective program, all the coaches must share a certain level of respect for one another and operate on the same frequency. The varsity coach controlled the overall program, and while I was coaching my own team, I still fell under the umbrella of someone else's vision. I disagreed with a lot of on and off the court philosophies. I refused to be marginalized as a coach and as an individual, which would never coincide with the desires of this program. Part of me was discouraged for the way things ended, but I was still a substitute teacher and could not have predicted the blessings God had around the corner. As my mother says, "No one can stop what God has for you."

June 7th, 2015: I was reading an article in the New Yorker about a young man by the name of Kalief Browder. I had never heard of this young man before, but seeing the years of his short life—1993 to 2015—displayed across my home screen as I opened the internet browser enticed me to learn more about this young brother. I read his story in utter shame and disbelief that our justice system was so corrupt, intentional, and fractured. Kalief was held in Rikers Island at the age of sixteen for allegedly stealing a backpack. He spent three years in prison, two of which were spent in solitary confinement—for a crime he did not commit. He was arrested for simply fitting a description, walking home from a party, engaging in normal teenage activities. During his time at Rikers, he suffered horrific physical and mental abuse at the hands of the inmates and prison guards. Kalief was not able to mentally recover from the trauma he faced in prison. Upon his release, he ultimately took his own life at the age of twenty-two. The weight of Kalief's story is something I have failed to lift from my heart. I searched my social media apps and found minimal chatter about this young man and his story. As with Mike Brown, Tamir Rice, and Freddie Gray a voice inside of my mind, heart, and spirit encouraged me to speak. No, I may not be able to inform the entire world about Kalief, but I can educate the individuals around me, and I can do all I can, where I am, with what I have. I posted a lengthy message on social media about Kalief and included a link to his story in the New Yorker. The feedback I received from my followers was overwhelmingly positive. I engaged in essential conversations about our justice system and my lack of faith in it. When you realize that terms "all men are created equal" and "equal protection under the law" were never intended to include people of color, the loopholes within the infrastructure becomes apparent. Why would the country hold these officers and positions of authority accountable for harming citizens they never intended to protect?

I began to feel a passion and conviction conversing about these issues, and it was unlike anything I had ever felt before. I became known for using my social media outlets to speak about the current issues within our country: from the Charleston nine, to Sandra Bland, to the voter ID laws, and new restrictions attempting to strip minorities of our right to vote, after loosening the protection of the Voting Rights Act of 1965. The more I discussed these tragedies, the more I educated myself on the inner workings of our society and the individuals who had dedicated their lives to exposing it, such as Charles Hamilton Houston, Malcolm X, Fred Hampton, and Angela Davis. I began to take from each one of these individuals the knowledge they left behind. While connecting with parts of their lives I identified with, and using that inspiration as a catalyst in my life in my own way, my adaptation continued by making the youth my priority.

Because I had now built a reputation for being vocal towards social and political issues, I was asked to speak at a Layman's League event, where numerous rising freshman receive scholarship money to attend college in the fall. I reluctantly agreed, not because I did not want to share my message, but because this was my first public speaking engagement and my nerves are wrecked. Speaking in front of a large audience was one of the biggest fears in my life, which was why I finessed the system and took my required public speaking course online in college. Although I was petrified, it was a positive sign that I accepted the invitation, willing to conquer that fear and anxiety. I started to write my speech a week before the event, but I could not seem to access the depths of my intellect. One speech was to dull, one was to militant, and one was uninspiring. Two days before the event, I still had not written a speech. I began to panic as doubts seeped into my brain. I took a walk around my neighborhood, searching for clarity. I recognize that I was putting entirely too much pressure on my own shoulders trying to find the perfect thing to say so I did not feel like I dropped the ball, like I failed to rise to the occasion. This message was not for me to receive. Those young students would be yearning for something organic to jumpstart them on their path to greatness, and there was nothing more genuine than a message from the heart. Not perfectly packaged, not over analyzed. I sat at my kitchen table that night and let my heart flow threw my hand. I was ready to deliver my first public speech.

As I approached the podium, I discreetly took several deep breaths, peering out at the sea of students (okay it was like ten total, but it felt like a thousand), their families, and members of my tribe. I smiled at the director who delivered my introduction. Sensing my nervousness, she offered a polite wink and head nod. I relaxed, took my leap of faith, and began to recite my speech:

Layman's League Speech
August 31st, 2015
Asheville, NC

Good evening everyone,

I am glad to see all of you here. First and foremost, I want to give all glory and honor to God for allowing me to be here this evening, and I am grateful for the opportunity to uplift and encourage our youth, the next generation of young minds.

It is important to understand that your time in college will be the best, but also one of the most challenging, times of your life. You will meet new people and build new friendships, but you will also meet individuals that will be able to help you with your career path in the future. Embarking on this journey is also preparing you for the real world. It's going to be times that you may feel lost or confused about what path to take and whether that path is what is best for you. During these times, as well as others, I advise you to lean on your faith and your family and understand that God has a plan and a higher purpose for your life. Maintain a positive outlook and never let anything discourage you. When I speak to my youth, I always tell them, God's will, will never take you where His grace won't protect you. This time will also be challenge for your parents. With you being away from home, it's only natural that they worry, "I hope my child is doing what they are supposed to be doing!" But the bible says in Proverbs 22:6, "Train up a child in the way he should go and when he is old he shall not depart from it." As a college graduate, I can assure that there were many times I had to refer to the morals my mother, my grandmother, my aunt, and my uncles all instilled in me, as well as the many lessons I received from my church family—which is the very foundation of our community.

College will teach you a lot of life lessons, but two of the most important ones are responsibility and accountability. As soon as your loved ones drop you off on campus, every action you take, every decision you make, is your responsibility. It becomes your responsibility to go to class and take your studies seriously. Have your fun and your time to turn up, but take your classes seriously. Realize how blessed you are to be receiving scholarship money and the opportunity to further your education, when our ancestors were denied the right to even pick up a book. That reason travels deeper than the color of our skin. It's power in the liberation of your mind and the freedom of your intellect. That is something that no man or woman can control or take from you. The great Charles Hamilton Houston said, and I quote, "The important thing is that no negro tolerates any ceiling on his or her imagination." I don't care whether it is your professor or your school advisor, never let anyone marginalize your impact.

The great leaders of our culture, Fredrick Douglass, W.E.B Dubois, Dr. King, Malcolm X, all had one thing in common, and that was the quest for knowledge to break the chains of the oppressor and mental colonialism. They liberated themselves not only for personal reasons, but for the betterment of our people and our culture. Brother Malcolm stated, and I quote, "You are not going anywhere in this world without an education." Take the time to educate yourselves on our history and where we come from as a people. If you don't know where you came from you, won't know when someone is trying to send you back. Part of being a great leader is how well you utilize your platform. Everyone in this room has a platform of some sort.

The question then becomes, what are you doing with yours? Don't be opposed to having a positive impact by getting out in the communities that surround your schools. You'll be surprised how many kids look up to you just because of the position you hold. I am sure there have been individuals in this room that have been inspired by someone. Don't be opposed to inspiring someone else.

In closing, I will say this, we are living in a critical time within the African American community. Our skin color is being weaponized by law enforcement so that we are no longer perceived as ever being unarmed. Some of our basic civil rights are being compromised; in this state, voting, specifically. We are fighting age-old stereotypes and systematic racism. The advancement of our people is extremely important. Every one of your young minds holds the key to our future, and we must take care of our own.

As I leave you tonight, during your time in college, I want you to remember these key points:

Lean on your faith and family

Have fun, but liberate your minds

Stay in school until you get your degree

Last, but not least, allow no ceilings on your a aspirations or margins on your impact

God bless you all, thank you.

It was an absolute honor and pleasure to deliver this speech about education and its significance. I never imagined

I would be someone who spoke to the hearts and minds of our youth, but this was just a testament to what God can do when you allow Him to take control while discovering your own light. The introvert in me, and the absence of self-pride, never allowed me to invite others into my true soulful spirit. I realized in doing that, I wasn't fulfilling my true purpose and properly using the platform God provided me with. Being a great basketball player was special, but it was not who I am. It was taking my platform and turning it into something bigger than a sport, turning it into something that could have an everlasting impact, because these ideals will live on long after the Lord calls me home. Proverbs 3:5-6 says, "Trust in the Lord with all your heart, do not lean on your own understanding. Seek his will in all you do and he will show you which path to take." The blessing lies in being able to truly understand what that means. This was only the beginning of what God had for me. My ascendency was nowhere near its peak, but trekking upward, I was ready to follow the direction of where His plan would guide me.

15

Hear my Prayer

In the immediate aftermath of my first speaking engagement, I felt myself becoming detached from basketball. I had little-to-no emotional attachment to the game and that thought brought satisfaction. There was a shift happening in my life and the information I provided transitioned further away from athletics. I sought the proper information needed to begin receiving my teaching certificate. I met with district administration and former educators to converse about the possibility of becoming a full-time teacher. Surprisingly, many of them expressed how they always believed I would end up in a classroom.

Days after I started to implement a plan of action of becoming a certified teacher, I was contacted by Asheville High School, who was searching for a girls' varsity basketball coach. They wanted to bring me in for an interview. I contemplated if this was an opportunity I wanted to pursue, as I felt my spirit disconnecting from basketball. Plus, Asheville High was the number one rival to my alma mater of TC

Roberson. In high school, I despised everything about Asheville High: the school, the coaches, the students, the facilities, everything. My most memorable games involved scoring twenty-five plus points in Asheville High's gymnasium in front of all their fans who pulled no punches when addressing my team and me. I considered how my community would view me. Would I be considered a traitor or disloyal to the TC Roberson community for joining a rival program? Or would the majority of the people understand a move of this magnitude?

I ultimately decided to go in for the interview, as I was anxious to receive information about the program, the future vision, and where I would fit into that picture. During our conversation, it was evident that this athletic department believed in my ability as a coach, stemming from my athletic background and observing the gradual improvement of my previous junior varsity team. As flattered as I was, I barely spoke about basketball. I reveal my true agenda from start. My players would be in weekly study halls, and I would be sending bi-weekly progress reports to their teachers. As a team, we would be involved in various community service projects and college prep activities to strengthen their character and place them in the best situations to attain higher education. I clarified that my philosophy transcended basketball, and I would not allow myself to exist only as an X's and O's coach. Two weeks following my interview, I was offered the job and I accepted. Although my growth was surpassing basketball, this was an opportunity too valuable to pass up. At twenty-four years old, I was handed the keys to an entire basketball program to shape and mold into importance. I could instill any plan, wish, or idea I had for my youth and was willing to protect that vision.

Before I accepted this job, I knew Asheville High was

amid rebuilding and that challenge was attractive to me. To establish complete and total change, you must first adjust the culture and alter the mentality of everyone who committed themselves to the system. I did not tolerate carelessness, tardiness, or giving me less than their best. This change was hard for my players to adapt to early on, but once they realized they could indeed execute what I demanded, the tide in their psyches swayed. No, we were not putting many W's in the win column, but these young ladies were accessing esteem and confidence that had not been discovered within them yet. We lost a lot of games early to talented and veteran teams, but my team remained committed to the process and locked into our collective goals.

My activism continued to grow alongside my coaching career, as I gave two more speeches based on black history and education shortly after the season officially started. However, I was careful about how I shared certain events with my team. Working within the school system, there are certain rules and guidelines you must follow as it pertains to the actions you take and what you verbalize to your players or students. Although there was nothing in the handbooks against formally speaking about social and political issues, I created a method that caught the eye of my team, but protected me in case someone from the outside saw my information as "problematic." If there was an act of police violence, a racial injustice, or an event that I felt my players needed to be made aware of, I would wear all black clothing during practices and games. This prompted them to ask questions about my choices and who I stood in solidarity with, sparking intellectual curiosity. I coached in all black to exemplify unification with "Concerned Student 1950" and the university of Missouri protesters who demanded their university offer consequences to assailants perpetuating racial intimidation on campus AND the administration who failed to produce reform. This demonstration had a profound impact on my players once they researched the circumstances surrounding the rebellion and discovered that the University of Missouri football players used their power to their advantage and refused to practice until Missouri's president resigned. This was the first indication to my team that athletes have the aptitude to use their voices and leverage against any injustice that speaks to their souls.

December 18th, 2015: I accompanied my mother to the doctor's office as she was scheduled to have her first colonoscopy. In the waiting room, she was fantasying about being able to go eat breakfast after the procedure was over, and we both agree that we will go to our favorite breakfast spot (Huddle House) once she was released. After she was called into the back, I waited thirty minutes until I was instructed by the nurse to come join her in recovery. They tapped my mom to wake her from her sleep. As the doctor entered the recovery room, he approached her with a terrible look of concern on his face. He informed my mom that he discovered a possible cancerous tumor in her colon that needed immediate attention. My mother and I locked eyes with each other and began to sob. The doctor tried to comfort us by saying, "Everything is going to be okay," but I could not get the echo of him telling us that my mother could possibly have cancer out of my head. The stench of those words was forever imprinted in my being. I stormed out of the room as he continued to speak with my mother. I have no idea what words were exchanged, I just knew I wanted to run, hide in a corner, and shrivel up to submerge in my emotions. Everything inside me wanted to crumble, but I realize that I had to stay vigilant for my mother. So, I made my best attempt to hold myself together.

After meeting with the surgeon, my mother was admitted to the hospital, scheduled for surgery the very next day. We were assured that the surgery was a very simple procedure and that the best plan of action would be mastered following the procedure. My grandmother and I shared the burden of informing my family of the news and everyone flocked to the hospital—including my brother, who grabbed an emergency flight from D.C. I had to inform my athletic director and mentor, who coached the boys' basketball team, of my mother's health, and they offered their love and support. We were scheduled to play a rival high school the same day and same time as my mother's surgery. The choice was clear to me; I would not be on that sideline coaching any game. When I told my mom of my plan to be with her, she continually objected, but I was not going to budge. So, I compromised instead. I stayed with her until she went into the room for her procedure, then went to coach my game. She made me promise to go stand on that sideline for her, and I did.

By the time tip-off occurred, the entire Asheville High community was aware of my mother's surgery and the outpour of prayers and support was overwhelming. When I stepped on the sideline, any pair of eyes could observe that my heart and mind where not in that gymnasium. I fought back tears on several different occasions during the game, and at one point, I just sat down on the bench, never uttering a word. We lost that game by thirty points, as I was in no mental or emotional place to helm my ship. I should not have coached the game to begin with, but I had to fulfill my promise.

When I returned to the hospital, I began to worry, as my mother had not yet come out of surgery. One hour turned into two, two turned into three, and three into four. In the early hours of the morning, the only people left in the hospital waiting room were members of my tribe. At 2 am, the surgeon entered, and for a moment, I felt as if time had stopped. The pounding of my heart eliminated my senses, and I braced myself for whatever news he was about to deliver. He explained that my mother's condition was far more extensive than anticipated. He was able to remove the entire tumor, but it was indeed cancerous. By his initial findings, he believed that she had stage 3 or 4 colon cancer. The room became completely silent. All I heard was the faint cries of my family. I cried silently as I fell into the arms of my aunt, who squeezed me as tight as she could. My brother's pain was manifested through anger as he forcefully pushed the double doors open to exit the waiting room. One of my aunts, who is a doctor, began to ask questions about the prognosis, and after I heard the word 'chemotherapy', I tuned the rest of the conversation out. I sat in shock as I was forced to wonder if I was about to lose my best friend, my backbone, my joy, and the queen of my life. That thought sent a shock of fear and sorrow through my body unlike anything else I've every experienced. As my brother rejoined us, he pulled me aside, with red eyes, and told me that no matter what happened, our mom was going to need us to help her get through this. Now, the roles had been reversed. It was my turn to be my mother's strength and backbone, to nurse her back to health.

I took a three-week leave of absence from my coaching duties as my mom recovered from her surgery. When she heard about her diagnosis, her reaction petrifies me. The hardest words I have ever heard my mother say were, "I need to start making plans." To watch this woman, who had been so durable, energetic, and tenacious all her life, find herself staring down a life or death obstacle, terrified of what was to come, was absolutely crushing. My brother and I created a system of trading off time at the hospital to ensure each of us could get proper rest—which did not come easy. Having to stay positive and upbeat while facing the possibility of losing your mother was a burden I did not know if I could carry. I spent hours upon hours praying to God that my mom survive this and praying for the strength and restoration, each hour of each day, to be the other crutch she could lean on.

I also prayed that my mother could exude her own faith for the benefit of her mental and spiritual nourishment to fight the good fight. As news spread about my mom's diagnosis, countless phone calls, text messages, emails, and social media posts flooded my cell phone from numerous individuals. From childhood friends, college teammates, and the Asheville community, to people I had not seen or heard from in years offering prayers, love, and support. The silver lining in her diagnosis was the unity she brought to so many people. My team played three games in the first week of my absence, winning two out of the three. They called me after each win to tell me they were playing for my mother and me, but also to inform me that after talking to our athletic director, our team grade point average was a 3.8 for the semester, and two of our seniors were accepted into their top choices for college. I dared not conceal how special these young ladies made me feel. I was somebody to them, as hard as I pushed them and challenged them. In my greatest time of need, their simple concern gave me an extra boost. These young women bought into my system and believed in my message of education over all, and it paid dividends for each one of us.

Days after her surgery, the plan for her chemotherapy schedule was revealed. We now knew the steps we had to take to ensure her healing. The mood was somber, until my mother looked at my brother and I and said, "I'm gon' be all right!" in the best version of her Kendrick Lamar voice she could muster. The strength we were trying to offer, my mother still possessed. We were broken, but not beaten. Our spirits remained high, ready to grab each other by the hand and walk with the Creator through our toughest journey to date.

In the coming months, I realized that there was no amount of preparation I could have gathered for this terrain. My brother returned to D.C, visiting once a month for a week at a time, and that left me as my mother's primary caregiver for the first three months of her chemo. Though spirits were high, things were not easy. My mom dealt with sickness after the removal of her pump every other week, and there were times when she would just lay down and repeat, "Baby, I am tired. I'm so tired," wanting to give up. I wanted to give into the part of me immersed in torment, but I snapped out of my trance when I remembered that my mother needed me, and her mental stability mattered more than my own because staying mentally encouraged was an important piece of the battle. Managing an entire basketball program on the back end of this personal challenge was strenuous when I returned, but with the assistance of my tribe and the cooperation of my players, coaching my team became my outlet. Even still, I continued to move further and further away from the game of basketball.

On Dr. Martin Luther King Jr.'s national holiday, I wrestled with the idea of canceling practice, instead going to participate in local holiday programs. The problem was, we are scheduled to play the number one team in the conference the following day, and I was not completely comfortable sending my team into that big of game unprepared. So, I scheduled practice for the early afternoon, but required my players to report to the gym at 10am to watch "Selma"—the film based on the fight for voter's rights and protection in 1965, Selma, Alabama; it was directed by the beautiful and radiant visionary, Ava DuVernay. Since we were in a position where we had to practice, I made sure that my team understood the significance of this day and how it directly affected them right now.

After we watched the movie, I had a lengthy conversation with them about what they saw. We were reminded of the people who fought, bleed, and died for our basic civil rights. Many were introduced to Jimmie Lee Jackson, Andrew Young, and the iconic John Lewis. We now had the luxury to be able to vote without a literacy test, poll tax, and without needing to travel to a polling location without the threat of paying the ultimate price. It's the little things we often take for granted, but these individuals portrayed in Selma, and films like it, fought for these rights, knowing they may not live to see the day these changes would occur. Regardless, they did it for us, and now it was my turn to do it for them. My team had little-to-no knowledge about the Voting Rights Act being compromised and how it affected their ability to register to vote. I explained to them that their voice and opinions were always valid, and if they connect with a cause, they deserve to be heard. This action did not sit well with some people outside of my program.

Being an athlete or involved in sports at any capacity, if you are outspoken about topics or events that do not have anything to do with sports, some individuals use your athletic ability and knowledge to place the stain of, "Stay in your lane and entertain me" upon you. I allowed that to happen once, and I would not allow it to happen again. I carried an idea of liberating young black minds and upliftment, not one of malice or disrespect. Where some individuals would like for these children to stay unexposed to their own empowerment, I had a hand in their discovery. Being secure in my conviction prevented anyone from telling me what avenue I can and cannot travel. No one can halt what I am inspired and called to do. I would have failed at my job as a basketball coach if my players could only refer to something I taught them on the basketball floor. Life does not end when the last buzzer sounds, and I became unapologetic in this message. My team telling me about what universities they applied to and had been accepted to, their aspirations of becoming doctors, physical therapists, and business women was the biggest win for me at the conclusion of each week. These facts forced me realize that the flame burning in my heart for basketball was nearly extinguished.

For the remainder of the season, I struggled with the feelings of maintaining an occupation that I had no desire of keeping. I simply did not want to be in a gym anymore or be around a basketball. The only people that brought me back each day were my kids. When I saw them, I suppressed my internal feelings of wanting to move on and dedicated myself to that practice or that game. I was living out my ambitions of bringing more attention to education and our social climate, and it brought me happiness; something I was no longer feeling as a coach. I felt the urge to entirely exclude sports from my life. I planned a fundraiser to send aid to the residents of Flint, Michigan. I also wrote an opinion piece in the local newspaper about the attempt to undermine the Black Lives Matter movement, went into after school programs, and volunteered at high school tutoring services to assist with the development of our young people. I wanted a position that could suit me for the person I was and the passions I harbored. Basketball was a thing of my past that my grown-self no longer connected with. There were things within this country and my community that I could not accept, and it was now time to elevate my platform to a level that athletics would have never accomplished. The spirit of God, in the form of the wind, He showed me that it was time to take another step forward in my purpose.

17

Black Woman at Work

I used the summer to reflect on my life. By the end of August, my mother had been declared cancer free as she finished her chemo regime. She now aimed to regain her strength. I considered the direction I intended to travel. My decision to step away from coaching was effortless. I kept my players in mind, but they deserved someone who would be willing to commit to them through basketball as their coach, and I was no longer that person. Being an athlete gave me an influence that I came to embrace, and that affect would not disappear once I completely removed myself from sports. I am forever indebted to what the game gave me and the position it placed me in, but my passion vanished and my fire has burnt out. I closed the book on basketball, forever.

The summer provided me with ample time to create a few community projects as well as search for an occupation that combined education and the advancement of the people. The first project I executed was a door-to-door voter's registration drive in my neighborhood. I did not want a huge event with incentives to entice the people to come to a central location. No, I was bringing my information to their front door. A small group of volunteers and I split up and covered the entire Shiloh community in half a day. We discussed the voter suppression and the need for every individual in our community to be aware of the reduction of early voting days, same day registration, and being unable to vote without a photo I.D. These were deliberate measures to discourage the black and brown vote. My purpose for pounding the pavement, in the literal sense, was to illustrate that no matter what constraints were placed upon us, we would not be intimidated or underrepresented at the polls.

The major victory of this day occurred when I came across a brother that was recently released from prison. When I explained to him why I was on his front porch and the meaning behind my mission, he said politely, "What you are doing is great, but as a convicted felon, I cannot vote." As he spoke to me, the trouble of his past weighed on him as he reflected on how one bad decision cost him five years of his life and his civil rights. I asked if he was done serving his time or if he was on probation, and he said he was not. I relay to him that in North Carolina, his voting rights were restored upon his release and all he had to do was re-register. This brother was not aware that he could reclaim his voice in this world and right there on his front porch, he reclaimed his rightful place in our society. The cause God placed on my heart was bigger than myself; it was about the progression of the people.

Once I squared away the young adults and elders, I turned my attention to our future, our children. Mere weeks from returning to school, I scrambled to think of a way to elevate them going into a brand-new school year. After several hours of brainstorming, I contacted a childhood friend who was a barber and we agreed to collaborate on a free back-to-school event entitled, 'Cutz for Class'—providing the youth in Shiloh and surrounding communities with free haircuts, school supplies, and a free lunch. Once my brother and I began to promote the event, it sparked others to want to get involved. We received donations from multiple people throughout the city and our tribe stepped up and volunteered.

What started as an idea between two individuals, evolved into an entire community effort. Our local news outlet came and conducted an interview about why we would want to do something like this and my answer was simple: *"This is where we are from. We grew up in Shiloh, we love Shiloh, and the sense of community here is amazing. Now that we are college graduates who are back home, we wanted to do something to uplift, specifically, our youth to show them that we care about our own, and we are here to guide them into success."* I was calculated in my approach, and exact in what I wanted to say. Unlike a year and a half ago when excitement skewed realism and I allowed a false depiction of the area, I controlled the narrative within this story and proudly displayed the sincere portrayal of my people. Seeing the light in the children's faces and the appreciation from their parents and grandparents compelled us to bring more events of significance to everyone.

I accepted a media assistant position at a local elementary school to ensure a steady income while I continued my search for the ideal position. It was not completely distant from where I wanted to be, since it was education driven, but it was not my target age group. Working with elementary age students is very challenging, especially when you must dilute your intellect to convey a message in a way that the young students can understand. My place of employment had a solid percentage of African American babies, but lacked inclusion to parallel that number. I identified this early as I met new staff members and felt a mutual attraction with these students. Being in a flexible position, I could float in various classrooms and interact with different students, again utilizing my strength in my ability to connect with the youth.

I assisted teachers who asked if I could spend extra time with students who needed help in reading and comprehension, as well as students that could be "troublesome"—in need of a role model. I thought about how I could empower these students, particularly the older ones, so I asked them who their heroes were. I found it problematic that every person they named was an athlete or entertainer. When I questioned them on if they had heard about Dr. King, Malcolm X, and the leaders of the Civil Rights Movement or other important African American people, their answers wavered. Fridays were our opportunity to wear "causal" clothing, so I used it to my advantage by displaying an image of iconic African people to spark the interest of, "Who is that?" "What did he or she do?" and "Why are they dressed like this?" It worked well with the children, as their decisions in the books they picked and what they wanted to learn slowly began to shift. Instead of grabbing three football and basketball books, it was now two baseball books and one history based book. Some staff members loved what I brought to the school and their students, others felt threatened by my "In your face" pride of self.

Being African American in the workforce, you must learn how to maneuver and exist in an infrastructure that may not be completely inclusive and is made up of a structure that was not built by us. Contrary to what people are willing to admit, educated and outspoken African American men and women can make people uncomfortable because we are a peril to the status quo. We should be able to be ourselves in the workplace, but the reality is, we cannot do so without the risk of making colleagues "uncomfortable." If we have a laid back and quiet demeanor, it is often misread as having an attitude or feeling that we are superior. I personally had the challenge of overly stepping out of my natural self to appease others, to the point that it was not authentic. Completing the duties of my job, being cordial and friendly, engaging in conversations when they were necessary and genuine should have been enough. In addition to carving out our deserved space in the workforce, we have the test of how to handle professional concerns and problems with coworkers or superiors. We must mindful of how we verbalize our treatment or situations of distress because people are quick to label one as being "angry," or we are expected to let these things go, invalidating our feelings. I worked beside several individuals, in my short time in the professional world, who knowingly or unknowingly questioned my competence through assignments I received, subsequently micromanaging my every move. That can create an antagonistic atmosphere that we, as African Americans, cannot always debunk; and that is unfair.

Just like I was unprepared for the system that college presented me, I found myself in a similar situation in the workforce, by not having these conversations before I accepted my first job. I zeroed my vison on being the best I could be for the students and positively influencing them. I did not have a second thought about how the method would affect the faculty because of what it was rooted in. I laid my best hand upon the table and the wrong individuals gained insight. I received a rude awakening about the methodical barriers placed around minorities in the workplace. I was living lessons, instead of learning them first, and it all circled back to my training and preparation. I vowed that no student to cross my path would wander into each tier of their lives, blindly. It was a heavy burden to carry, but black people must be ultra-prepared for anything. Even if you come into an occupation with the necessary knowledge and training, you will still face obstacles that most people do not see. The difference will be your reediness to identify and overcome. We are forced, particularly black women, to live with the idea that, if someone is giving 100%, you must give 110%; yet and still, working twice as hard for half as much. That is a disheartening reality to accept, with the expectation that we must be "perfect."

Because I was still searching for the ideal job for me, I was forced to stay level headed and preserve through these revelations. As frustrating as it was, I had to keep in perspective that there was a purpose behind all of this and the aspirations and possibilities of my future kept my perspective positive. I searched for different outlets of expression to decrease the stress I felt in this job, and writing became one of them. The more I wrote about these different experiences I have had—not only in the workforce, but over the entirety of my life—the more I sought to observe my reflection in the things that interested me, such as literature, film, television, and entertainment. Reading and writing developed into more than just a stress reliever. I found joy in my expression through poetry and small articles. My attention lasered on the creation of my interests, intriguing me to think about the possibility of my verbalization becoming visual to others, through several outlets. I searched for individuals who had a similar background and had followed the same path I had taken.

Paul Robeson was a name I heard on several occasions throughout my life, but sufficient time was never spent on his story. I was only provided with an overview of him being a star athlete who later changed the world through theatre. Upon studying his life and experiences, he represented the idea of who I was supposed to be. A star athlete, who was a valedictorian, and took his status and stature to new heights in order to leave an everlasting mark on this earth. His belief that African Americans should distinguish themselves in a variety of realms, to show that we are capable of anything, spoke to me as I saw and felt his impact in sports, education, law, activism, theatre, and film. He was an athlete first, but that is the last thing you remember about him because he has accumulated so much, over a broad scope.

Looking at the creations I have kept close to my chest at this point, experiencing this renaissance type period of African American narratives, shared throughout numerous outlets, sparked a desire to study more about athletes who have made transitions into various avenues. Nnamdi Asomugha is another individual that I looked upon and discover that he created a blueprint on how to be an ex-athlete transitioning into your best life. He is an ex NFL pro bowler who has produced several life changing films and starred in a few as well. Nothing about him creating these stories felt forced or random because he approached this passion in the same way he did the one of old. He created a foundation that serves underprivileged youth who aspire to attain a higher education. Nnamdi is another example of an athlete expanding their original platform into much more than what was formally envisioned. Exposing myself to these exceptional stories and leaders of the past and present, in addition to discovering a personal pursuit by tapping into everlasting creativity, produced a perfect storm and stretched my message and purpose.

I was contacted by a school counselor at TC Roberson high school who ran a leadership club for African American and Hispanic students. I was asked to give a speech about college, education, and its importance as it related to these students. By this time, I had several speaking engagements attached to my resume, and these events had become second nature. My appearance was scheduled for November 11th, three days after our presidential election. I wrote my speech a week prior to ensure I was prepared to share some of my experiences as a college student and what helped me in my transition from a careless athlete to a conscientious educator.

The aftermath of November 8, 2016 altered my entire speech, and I was frightened—not only by the country electing a demagogue, but the fact that I was going to have a room full of black and brown children looking to me for some of sort of sign that everything would be alright. As intimidating as the thought was, again, God placed this opportunity in my path, at this time, with these young people, for a reason.

I did not write a new speech until the morning of my appearance. I wanted to sit with all the emotions of the direction the country was heading and deliver a heartfelt message. When I walked into the classroom, I could feel the blanket of disappointment and uncertainty. These students were having a rough time trying to understand why this happened and what it meant for them moving forward. During the reading of my introduction, I fell into a quick prayer, simply asking God to move through my mind and body to deliver the message He intended to be heard. Here is what I said:

Empowerment Speech
November, 11, 2016
T.C Roberson High School
Asheville, North Carolina

"Good morning young brothers and sisters. It's an honor to be visiting with you this morning, to offer a little knowledge and exchange wonderful ideas with you young people. I was invited to speak with you about preparing yourselves for college, the benefits of higher education, and to share a few of my experiences as a college student and athlete, and how all of this directly contributed to the adult you see standing before you. This will not be the basis of my message to you all today, as you and I have been presented with the Trump era. I pray you hear my words, latch onto what empowers you, and leave this space encouraged.

I assume that you all have joined this club because you want to move forward into college and obtain your bachelor degrees. That's great, and this is the first major step along your route to prosperity. This is the moment when you say to yourself, "I want more for my life, I want to set my sights high, and place myself in a position to accomplish the highest peak." What you do during your time in high school is building a foundation you will carry into transition as a college student.

The best way to enter a college or university ahead of the curve is to equip yourself with as much information as you can prior to your move in day. It is important to have a few ideas of what career you want to establish post-graduation and research the universities that support those aspirations, including their application and acceptance requirements—such as GPA and standardized testing scores. Learn how to build relationships with some of your high school teachers so you can use them as references. Make them want to write you a letter of recommendation, based off your overall behavior and respect. Doing this now develops a good habit of being able to connect with individuals who are in a position to help you along the way. Build your resume by seeking volunteer opportunities based on something you enjoy doing or want to bring a change to.

As high school students, there are already younger children who look up to you simply because of where you are in your life. It's important to make sure the next generation knows they are worthy. Volunteering creates a selfless and appreciative attitude, while providing these institutions with evidence of what you will bring to their college or university. Give them insight on how you could serve the surrounding community of their school.

It is pivotal to remember that simply being able to converse about this process and having this opportunity is both a privilege and a necessity. If it was not, we would not have been denied this right centuries ago. Someone sacrificed for you to sit in these chairs, to break down the barriers they dedicated their lives to. There is a reason that some of your parents, grandparents, uncles, aunts, elders, and various members of the community drill the idea of education into your brain. They emerged from the segregation era, they had a firsthand view of inequality through education, and now that you do not have that dark cloud over your head, they want you to take full advantage of the opportunities they were denied.

Once you embark on your colligate pathway, the hurdles will begin to present themselves. You have to adjust to having a lot of free time and no one instructing you on how to use it. College will be one of the best periods of your life: seeing new places, meeting new friends, expanding on experiences, and partaking in the parties that are on a different level! You are supposed to involve yourselves in the fun activities that come along with being a college student, but never forget why you are on that campus—your education. Observing my friends and fellow students in college, I realized that the people you associate with are the individuals you choose to be your family. So, be mindful of the company you keep. Surround yourself with friends that intend on achieving their goals just as much as you do. You are already labeled with the low expectations society has for you, never allow you or your friends to wear those tags.

Academically, the best advice I will offer you is to create relationships with the administration of your department, academic advisors, and administrative branches that offer internships. This is critical for your post-graduation life because I am living proof of someone who did not seek this information, and it made my job search a harder because I entered the job field with absolutely no experience. So, handle your business in the classroom and search for outlets that will put you ahead of requirements when it is time for you apply for an occupation.

All of what you choose to do rests solely on your shoulders. Do not arrive with the expectation that your professors, advisors, or athletic coaches (for those who may play college sports) will monitor you and keep you from steering down the wrong path, and it is going to present itself at some point. When you come to that crossroad, be sure you have fed yourself the proper conviction to stay the course towards everlasting peace and prosperity. As I carry with me, throughout the city, some of you have heard my other speaking engagements that proper education does not stop in a textbook that your school provides. A lot of our history is hidden, the best parts of our history. Empower yourself to find out why. I am a twenty-five-year old college graduate, and I discover something fresh about our history and contribution to this country daily. There is a new intellect, civil rights leader, doctor, lawyer, inventor, or event that I come upon, and it is shocking how much I did not know, but I realized why. All of these people and instances gave us hope, and there is nothing that can derail a person who has immense hope. This leads me to the final portion of my message.

It is okay to be saddened and disappointed in the wake of the election results. It is okay to feel the pain of America's defiance to an inclusive society, but we are not a people who walk in fear, and we cannot allow fear to occupy our space. Yes, young people, we have been faced with our biggest obstacle in this life, but we will not cower or flee. We will not accept his rhetoric or internalize the racism. We will resist and protect what is ours. We will endure and combat each marginalized box, conditioned in privilege, attempted to be placed on our people. We are still in control of the narrative for our lives, and each one of you students in this room has a voice. Embrace it all, your potential, your capability, your wit, your understanding, your black boy joy and black girl magic. Your perspective will change when you provide yourself with the context. Find your passion, develop your vision, and maintain your opposition against anything that further contributes to the disenfranchisement of the people. Never allow anyone to tell you that your empowerment equals hate, or that your assertiveness to say 'I matter', means that their life does not. The totality of equality has remained and forever will be the ultimate intention. Young brothers and sisters, find your light, and remember who's still in control. God bless each and every one of you, thank you."

After I conclude this speech, the blanket of disappointment I felt when I entered the room had been replace by enthusiasm. Several of the students walked up to me asking about books I had read and if my mindset has always been this way or was it something I learned. They had no clue that a mere three years ago, I was a shell of the person that stood before them today. The students expressed their appreciation for the words I shared, and I extended my social media information to a number of them. To this day, I remain in contact with all of those students who are now freshmen in college. The final portion of my speech was not written or rehearsed, as I purposely wanted my emotion and the wave of God to wash over me so that the students could see Him through me. I realized that the values I shared would live on through the children I planted these seeds in. There was no way to neutralize that. Our future remains in great hands.

In the weeks following the election, I noticed that non-minority individuals at my job and around the city of Asheville were wearing safety pins outside of their clothing and I could not figure out why. I logged into my social media pages and saw a flood of images with non-minority individuals with safety pins on their shirts. As I sought more information about the meaning of this, my spirit was bothered. It was my belief that the "Safety Pin" trick was ridiculously problematic. Not voting Donald Trump did not suddenly exempt these individuals from decades of beneficial systematic racism and privilege. Now, to presumably ease guilt, under the mask of, "I am safe, we can talk," you want to hear what minorities have been screaming for since the day we arrived off the boat? These safety pins illustrated to me that our voices were being heard, but the disruption of normalcy equipped some to cover their ears. This attempt at solidarity fell flat, and I refused to engage I conversations with individuals at my job or on social media that sought to speak about where our country currently stood.

Months later, when the women's marches occurred all over the world in protest of the president's inauguration, I was pleasantly satisfied with what I saw. The marches and illustration of resistance shown was one step toward the ultimate goal of equality for all. But, the true challenge was in, what happens next? Sustaining this action at every level, for all the citizens of this nation, would be key. The true work began after the march. People who had been on the front lines, on the ground, in the trenches for years, had to do more. The people who recently began to resist, had to march onward. The people, who had the state of this country weighing on their conscience, but chose to take comfort in normalcy, had to get up. My concern was moving forward. *How will we view each other? How will we incorporate each other? How and WILL we support each other in the various liberation movements?*

Everyone can make a difference, but this has to be continuous for all of us. Demonstrate and resist, not for you, but for your fellow humans who deserve an opportunity, inclusion, and protection. The road to be traveled will be met with enormous opposition, wills will be bent, faith will be tested. BUT God, and the desire for what is rightfully ours, will sustain us, and I believe the riches will be plenty. Firstly, your comfort has to be disrupted, your empathy must increase, and your knowledge must expand. You must start with your own bias (knowingly or unknowingly) and decondition yourselves from the societal shackles that keep us in a state of separation. We cannot dismantle a system until we dismantle ourselves.

While I was encouraged by the protests, the outcome remained to be seen, and again, I refused to converse about this topic in the workplace. I was silently frowned upon when I answered the question of whether I participated in the march with a simple 'no'. I did not see this largely diverse demonstration for Sandra Bland, Tanisha Anderson, or Yvette Smith. My skepticism was valid, because if part of what you are advocating for is "women's rights" and "racial equality," then explain why the magnitude of this demonstration did not happen for these women and others like them? This march was encouraging, but I was not a believer yet, and I was not in a position to completely explain this to my colleagues, because I am a black woman at work, who now understood the difficulties attached to that.

Four months into my job at the elementary school, in my continual search for a better position, a highly successful non-profit organization had an opening for a Athletics and Teen Program Development lead. I jumped at the chance to apply, as the basis of this position provided the freedom to create while combining my enthusiasm for the community. I was nervous when I completed the application because this job was tailor made for someone like me, and this could potentially be a life changing move. Weeks after submitting the application, I took part in a short phone interview which covered the basics of who I am in addition to a few open-ended questions. After the first step of the process went smoothly, I was scheduled for an in person, in-depth interview. This was when I took my biggest leap of faith. My job at the elementary school was solid, and I adored being able to work with those babies, but ultimately, it was not what I wanted to do, nor was it the position I wanted to be in. So after four months, I stepped down as the media assistant.

I stepped down without confirmation of a new job, but I was determined to land where my heart desired. I bet on myself, and I allowed God to take the lead. I approached my personal interview like it was my only hope, and it was, because I would be forced back to square one if this went left.

I was confident going into the interview. I knew I had the qualities necessary to be successful in this position. When the interview started, the very first question I was asked was, "We see that you have held several events in your community. Where does that passion stem from?" I exhaled, as I smiled and opened the floodgates of information and influence. We conversed about my aspirations, why this job attracted me, my athletic accomplishments, my published newspaper articles, and my future vision for the teenage population. It began to feel like a conversation of exchanged ideas rather than a formal interview. We spoke with one another for over an hour, and I exited that meeting feeling that this job was mine. I was comfortable, vulnerable, excited, and informative about who I was and what I strived to be.

I was growing increasingly nervous as the days continued to pass. I had conferring conversations with myself in my head. Yes, you read that right. I started examining the interview, wondering if I'd said too much or too little. Was I too militant? Did I clarify enough? A week and a half passed before I was contacted by the supervisor of the division. On March 28, 2017, I was offered the position of Athletics and Teen Program Development Lead. I became intoxicated with joy. All the searching, my professional journey, and seeking my lane in this world led to this moment. I was finally serene and content in my place amongst the world of professions.

'Job' is a cheap word to describe what I hold because there are profuse feelings absent of that. As a Teen Program Development Lead, under the umbrella of our non-profit, I have the responsibility of developing educational programs aimed at prepping teens for college and the workforce, in addition to bringing this information to underprivileged youth who aspire to further their education, but simply lack the resources and information on how to get there. My program partners with local business for my teens, to shadow them in various jobs, as well as provide them with an opportunity for summer internships. My volunteers and I provide weekly tutoring sessions, and leadership development during the school year for teenagers who attend the local high school we hold a partnership with. Monthly summits are held with a specific concentration rooted in college prep or workforce skills. We provide students with tours of local colleges and universities, including prestigious historically black colleges and universities, in addition to volunteering in numerous community projects. I make it a point to expose these young students to theatre, film, art, music, and literature through different activities I organize, never wanting to exclude any fraction of information to them, sparking the dream that will evolve into their reality. The day this job slid across my screen is the day my post-graduation journey made sense. My transition out of coaching and into education, using education as the basis of activism, and becoming selfless in what I give was experienced in its fullest capacity in this moment, and God was my orchestrator.

17

Maria

I was sitting on my grandmother's porch in reflection. I asked myself, *am I considered a success?* Then I asked myself, *well Maria, what is a success to you?* I redefined my world view of what it means to be a success and what it means to "make it." Do I possess a lot of riches in the world? No, but success is not measured by the material items you have. It is based on the jewelry you harbor on the inside. Lastly, I asked, *but, do the people know how you came to harbor those gems?* I started to think about all the speaking engagements and community events I'd conducted and gathered that I'd never voiced my story. Sure, I gave an overview of accomplishments before I went into sharing vital information, but I never verbalized what happened in my life that led me to this point.

That is a deep and partly unflattering story. I don't know if you should do that, I said to myself and timidly decided against it. Weeks passed as I remained indecisive about sharing so much of my personal life with the masses. But eventually, I began to write anyway and completed a piece that was a five-part article that could be published in a newspaper or magazine entitled, 'The Sunken Place of A Black Athlete.' The article reads as such:

SIGNING DAY

In April of 2009, I, Maria Young, signed a National Letter of Intent to play college basketball at Limestone College in Gaffney, SC. The seats in the gymnasium at TC Roberson High School in Asheville, NC were filled with my family and friends, as we all shared this incredible achievement. I heard everything from, "Go make history!" to "Don't come back to Asheville!" to "Don't squander this opportunity!" and lastly, "Make sure they remember your name when you leave," but I never heard, "Don't forget the real reason you are there."

LIMESTONE DAYS

During my time at Limestone College, I was a four-year starter and ended my career as the school's all-time leading scorer, (a record that has since been broken). There isn't much athletically that I have not accomplished, individually or with my team. I take pride in all of these accomplishments because I worked extremely hard to become a great basketball player, and I indeed "made history." Athletically, I soared as the accolades and recognition rolled in from the day I put on a Limestone basketball jersey. I was showered with admiration and praise every place I went, with everyone telling me how great my team and I were. My name and face could be seen on the news and in the newspapers in my hometown, as well as in the city of Gaffney. I had several write-ups about me as a basketball player in different outlets, national televised games, individual conference awards, conference tournament awards, and multiple NCAA tournament appearances.

I harbored a nonchalant attitude and possessed a feeling of invincibility based off my performance as an athlete. The danger is, if that feeling is not anchored in purpose, and humility has the power to detach you from reality. Off the court, life was simple—if it didn't pertain to the game it wasn't significant to me. Mistakenly, I viewed school as something I had to do in order to stay eligible, not as a pathway to endless opportunities. I took easier classes with a lower curriculum to receive a good grade. I would miss an 8 or 9 am class if it interfered with my rest prior to a game. I would not complete certain assignments until the day after a competition, no matter the due date. I was able to request that tests and quizzes be taken on a different date (some with penalties and some without), and I produced the bare minimum in my classes because I could, and it was expected of me. Embarrassingly enough, I allowed my peers and professors to enforce the stereotype of the 'black college athlete' upon me, and I existed in a marginalized box entitled, "athlete only." I never lacked the knowledge, want, or competence, but in this moment, it wasn't important enough to me.

MY MIND IN A "SUNKEN PLACE"

You ask, "How could you do that!" "How dare you be in that position and not take your education seriously?!" As an athlete, this secondary attitude to-

wards academics was effortless. I accepted a pedestal that was built throughout my lifetime, with every step being bound by the "value" of sports and every brick secured by the hope of where the game could take me. When the majority of the praise you receive over your lifetime co-exists with your athletic ability, your gratification and identity become simultaneous with the game. My mood and feelings were controlled by the bounce of the ball, the sound of a swish, and my success within athletics. My sport became who I was, and not something I did. Unknowingly, I was swept into a cycle of validation, and a box with limited ceilings.

I failed to understand it was coming from something that should have been an accessory in my life, not a necessity of my worth. We are given the title "Student-Athlete" thinking that our being will exist under both terms. In my case, I CHOSE one over the other. I CHOSE to dedicate the majority of my time to my sport. I CHOSE to miss class. I CHOSE to miss deadlines for assignments because I accepted what others normalized, and I internalized multiple boundaries. For a long time, I had a plan A and plan A only that was based off of athletics. I thought basketball was my identity, and I wasn't prepared for the system I'd inherited. I did not make choices for my future; I made choices for the moment. It was not my coach's responsibility, it was not my advisor's responsibility, and it was not my professor's responsibility; it was mine. I was supposed to prepare myself for this, and I was supposed to be the master of my journey.

BREAKING THE SPELL

It's important to understand the term 'choice' and realize how it coincides with preparedness. Once your loved ones drop you off on campus, every action you take and every decision you make is yours, and you have to deal with the positive or negative ramifications of that choice. In order to make the right choices and decisions, you have to be prepared and possess a clear understanding and an ability to study the cracks of the system you are joining.

The NCAA stands firm behind the term "Student- Athlete" and preaches the message of being a student first and an athlete second. What they don't like to share is that their institutions generate millions from athletics. So, they allow athletic departments and coaches (some, not all) to steer athletes into majors that virtually have no job fields. They hide behind the guise of making things easier for "you" in the moment, but in reality, it's all so you can remain eligible to perform athletically, which directly benefits them. Some of these people fail to realize, OR simply don't care, that this system is setting young athletes up for failure. Because once they graduate, what career field are they going in to? What professional skills have you equipped them with to be successful post-graduation? This is where preparedness and choice become a major factor.

As an athlete, if you and your family are prepared and informed before you sign that Letter of Intent, you have already broken a cycle of self-destruction, because you are primarily focused on what you can do academically, and your choices will be based upon what you want out of your life once you graduate. When I say inform, I mean taking it upon yourself to seek the information people do not want you to know. It's going to be easy to want to miss a class when you get back to campus in the early hours of a school night from an away game. It's easy to turn in assignments late when your professors give you a little leeway because you play basketball. It's easy to solely focus on athletics when the majority of your day, every day revolves around your sport. And, the easy path of this system presents itself for a reason. Yes, the system we exist in athletically, academically, socially, and politically is very flawed—a flawed system that hindered but never stopped, my ancestors from achieving things the world said were impossible.

My biggest regret living in a "sunken place," as a student and an athlete, was forgetting. Forgetting that I was standing on someone else's shoulders, forgetting that I walked down a path that was forged in suffering and pain, forgetting that I had a luxury that so many before me would die to receive, forgetting that we had to build our own institutions of higher learning in the face of a country that denied us our chance for an equal education, and forgetting who and what I was representing. On December 14, 2014 I graduated in my fifth year with a Bachelor's Degree from Limestone College. I walked across that stage and received my degree in front of my family and friends as they screamed "SHILOH" and shed tears of joy. I had attained my biggest accomplishment, an accomplishment that for so long felt like a fleeting illusion.

Staying an extra year in college was not easy to accept initially, but it turned out to be a blessing in disguise. In that fifth year, I had no basketball, no film sessions, no weight training, no conditioning, no skill development, no team building, no practice, and no games. My life took on a different pace, and I discovered new passions. Knowledge became addictive to me, like a child who had been deprived of candy. I began to read outside of my classes, books like the 'Miseducation of the Negro' by Carter G Woodson, 'The Souls of Black Folks' by WEB Dubois, and 'A Slave Narrative' by Frederick Douglass. My mind was awakened, my eyes were opened, and I felt as if God had given me new life without the shackles of false securities. In this fifth year, at twenty-two years old, I finally discovered Maria. I discovered my true strength, knowledge, power, intellect, influence, and belief in myself. I was already equipped to be great, and I didn't even know it.

At twenty-six, I am Teen Program Director, activist, and a community organizer who is still striving for higher education to receive a Master's degree in History and to become a teacher. My journey is not complete. The game I dedicated so much of my life to, that I have since distanced myself from, is the same game that's given me a platform to inspire and change lives. That is what it was always supposed to be.

PREVENTION
Young black athletes should be taught early in life that any sport they are participating in should always remain secondary to their education. Relatives, friends, coaches, and communities need to be mindful of the pedestal and praise they heap upon

a young athlete. It's okay to be proud of athletic accomplishments, but do not let that be the only admiration he or she hears. Teach them early that black excellence is represented in ways other than athletes and entertainers. We are represented as doctors, lawyers, engineers, teachers, professors, architects, writers, inventors, scientist, and entrepreneurs.

Young athletes, be aware of the "Sunken Place" of glory, appreciation, esteem, and confidence rooted in athletic achievement. Be in command of your journey. Don't be an athlete who is on campus to simply play sports; be a part of an educating class. Do not accept people's low expectations of your academic performance, and do not accept what is normal. Put your future first, pick a major that you desire, and not one that will suit you athletically. Be a part of a program that will set you on a path to a thriving career and open yourselves up to experiences outside of your teammates and athletics. Give yourself an option to do and be more. Do not allow "ease" to cripple your future and prevent you from taking command of your life outside of athletics, or preparing yourself prior to college. You have a responsibility to yourself to be the best you can be.

You also have a responsibility to lead by example and illustrate to the next generation that you can be a young black student who happens to excel athletically. Last, but certainly not least, never forget the ones who came before you, and think about the ones who will come after you. One day, the fans will stop cheering, the ball will stop bouncing, the last buzzer will ring, the sweat will dry, and the lights will go off. Don't let that be where your story ends.

After I completed this article, I was still hesitant about sharing it; although, it only provided slight insight into my life. One night, I was scrolling through my twitter app and saw that one of my favorite artists, by the name of Katie Boeck, had released a new song, 'Waiting for Rain.' When I clicked on the YouTube link, I discovered that she had written a description about the inspiration behind this record. She described her storm and personal transformation brought on by the loss of her father. This song was a testimony to the depths she came back from. An excerpt from verse two, removed any apprehension preventing me from sharing my story.

She sings, "*It's a clumsy climb to my higher place, but it all looks new with a bird's eye view and that's my saving grace. I'm calling me out, I'm turning around because I'm wise enough now to know my way. All of my dreams they've scattered like seeds and now I'm just waiting, waiting for rain.*" This verse ran parallel with where I was in my life, and to witness and experience the vulnerability of a person with her stature pushed me to understand that my story could provide the same feeling to someone else; even if it was only one person, it would be worth it.

On June 2, 2017, I released the above article in the sports blog of Asheville's newspaper. I prayed that the message would be received through the flaws, and the response was staggering. I was flooded with emails, Facebook messages, tweets and direct messages, texts messages, and phone calls from current athletes and their parents thanking me for sharing my story and information. Former athletes told me that I did not understand what I had just done by exposing people to the pitfalls that come with being an athlete, and that my "impact would last for years to come." I became emotional at several points throughout the day because the support and feedback was more than I could have imagined. Questions began to flood my inboxes, wanting to know more. I went into prayer, receiving conformation to the yearning in my soul. It was time to write a memoir.

At twenty-six years old, my story is still being written, and I experience personal growth and development daily. The errors of my past have provided everlasting life lessons, in addition to presenting me with obstacles in this new chapter. You may have noticed throughout the text that I have mentioned wanting to attend graduate school to become a teacher. My poor academic performance in undergrad has crippled my options and slashed my chances of acceptance, but I am determined to do everything in my power to attain my Master's degree. Although I can look back over my life and wish I had made better decisions when it came to the important choices that affected my future, I do not live with regrets. Everything I went through, the triumphs and the tribulations, was part of God's plan for my life, and I could not be happier with the young woman who wrote this book. That would not have been achievable without the experiences of my past.

View the following message with a delicate mind and a sound spirit:

Youth is not equivalent to immortality. If you make sound and conscience decisions early, you lessen your chances to be punished for them later. Do not put yourself in a position to NEED a second chance, but keep steady in the place to achieve everything you desire. Nothing can trap your mind, body, and spirit if you are vigilant. Carry humility in all that you pursue, and never anchor your worth in something that is fleeting. Always remain hopeful, as you limit yourself when you operate out of fear. In the book Job chapter 14 verse 1,

God already promises us that our time on this earth is limited, and there will be days full of trouble, but choosing to halt in the despair that finds you is the acceptance of immersing in pain. You can control your own narrative if it is anchored in authenticity; redemption is always possible.

Your strength is forever renewed in the Most High when you place your worry and cares into His hands and place your life in His unconditional love. Every closed door is a test of your faith, but is not a rejection. It's simply a diversion into a blessing God has waiting for you. The day you discover your purpose, is the day your life has new meaning. Assist others in their quest for something similar. We are all blessed with a life worth living. Appreciate where you are in your life, growth happens even when you are not completely aware of it. Feel satisfaction in what you have, while aspiring for more. Do not allow anyone to marginalize any idea that you want to come to fruition. Your ambitions are valid; seek to be present in multiple avenues and protect your vision.

Be open to new ideas and experiences, remembering that when you are faced with someone different, it does mean they are deficient or inadequate. Connect with the vibes or a person, not their appearance, and listen to an individual's intent beyond face value. There is no need to tear down what you do not understand. Make a conscience effort to uplift someone on a daily basis through kind words or a good deed. You may never be aware of what a person is grappling with, and your generosity may serve as the strength they need to get through the day. BE the example of the change you want to see. Everyone can do something from where they are, with what they have. Realize that your life is unfulfilling when you are a self-servant. The power lies within the people. Use your God-given gifts to heal and unite.

I am sharing and building something that will outlive me; that is what makes me a success. The young child damaging her own light out of fear of what it would bring, now sees a twenty-six-year-old brilliant black queen who has found her peace in God's love. I cannot predict the future, or the good Lord's plans for me, but I can say that I am prepared for what is next, and I will continue to live my best life. May yours be long and prosperous.

Acknowledgements

First and foremost, as always, I will give all praise, glory and honor to my Lord and Savior, Jesus Christ for His many blessings of the past and all He has yet to do. Without God's grace and mercy, I would not have the strength to share this story with you all.

To my beautiful mother, my backbone, my rock, and my best friend. I could live a thousand years, with a thousand thank you's upon my lips and it would still fall short of my appreciation for your life. You are a true warrior and the blueprint of what a mother should be. To the rest of my family—my brother, cousins (who are more like my siblings), aunts, uncles, and grandmother thank you for your love, support, and guidance throughout my twenty-six years. It truly takes a village to raise a child, and I am blessed that God chose you as my tribe. When I fall, you pick me up, and when I succeed, you lift me up. I love each one of you.

To my father, the ride has been uneasy, only god knows what the future holds, but in this moment I thank you.

To my tribe of kinfolk, childhood friends, and college teammates, thank you for the purity of your friendships. So many of you have had a hand in my development and have shown me what true, everlasting kinship is supposed to feel like.

There is no success without your love, and tough love, at times. I am forever in debt to each of you. No matter where life takes us, we will always and forever remain family.

To my college coaching staff, thank you for never giving up on me through my countless mistakes and bad choices. You saw something in me that I did not have the power to see in myself until later in my life, but the blessing lies in the fact that you guys gave me something to refer to. My days playing for you in a Limestone College jersey were some of the best days of my life, and I would not have been the player I was without you on the sideline. I love you forever.

To Kennisha Thornton and the Nyree Press family, thank you for believing in me and the vison. Your assistance and generosity throughout this entire process has been magnificent. I am forever grateful for the opportunity you gave me to write my first book. It has been a thrilling experience.

To my young brothers and sisters, thank you for giving me purpose. I will continue to fight with you and for you in solidarity until the Lord calls me home.

Last, but certainly not least, Shiloh. Shiloh. Shiloh. One of the great joys of my life is being able to say I am from Shiloh. Thank you for showing me what a real community is and what it means to have pride in where you come from.

To my readers, thank you for embarking on this tremendous ride of emotions with me. Prayers of love, peace, health, healing, restoration, and prosperity to you. Stay righteous. I love you to life!

THE GOOD ONES

Some come in your life for seasons

God has his reasons

Every letdown holds a lesson

Pain becomes blessings

You appreciate the good ones

Accepting who they are

Without paying for the mistakes of some

How to know if you got a good one?

If they love you despite you

Then you've got one

CPSIA information can be obtained
at www.ICGtesting.com
Printed in the USA
BVHW040820110620
581031BV00004B/128